Persevere to Succeed

A Practical Guide to Ignite the Fire of Success Through Uncertainty

Amy McCann

Persevere to Succeed
A Practical Guide to Ignite the Fire of Success Through Uncertainty

ISBN 978-1-941852-21-7 (paperback)
ISBN 978-1-941852-25-5 (ebook)

Cover image © Denis Belitskiy | Dreamstime.com
Cover design: Heart of Jupiter Publishing

This book is dedicated to my beautiful daughters,
Emma and Annalise,
my solid and supportive parents, Marie and Bill,
the McCann siblings, for which this book is special and dear to my heart,
to my calm and loving husband Sean,
and my best friend for life, Susan.

CONTENTS

PREFACE

How often do you wish for better things to come your way? Are you disappointed when it doesn't happen? My favorite childhood fictional frog, Kermit, said it best when he asked, "Who said that every wish would be heard and answered?" in the famous song, *Rainbow Connection.* This introspective frog ignites his curiosity to ask, "What's so amazing that keeps us stargazing?"

Yes, what is so amazing that keeps us stargazing beyond our present struggles in hopes that we'll find answers? What compels us to keep going even if we don't have all the answers and even if our prayers are never answered? This is the human spirit, seeking to feel, do, and be more beyond killing checklists and meeting deadlines. Meaningful reflection and contemplation are where the entire body, mind, and spirit come together to actively stir up positive energy. It is our human nature to question, and apparently it is the nature of frogs, too!

As life gets busier and busier, we lose connection to any greater questions we might ask that could keep us from emotionally burning down or drowning the spirits with which we were blessed. We effectively deaden our curious natures about who we are, how we want to contribute, and what is most meaningful to us. We take no action to reprogram or make a change because we fear uncertainty. We usually react rather than pause. We gripe rather than act to ignite progress. Then, we eventually collapse in wonder of what may have gone wrong.

To succeed through and beyond uncertainty is to learn to persevere without self-sacrificing your health. It is to nourish the entire whole of ourselves. It is to see with eyes open the stars of faith and possibilities. Persevere to succeed, and you'll once again become curious about who you are on the inside. You'll have no need to wish for all the answers to life's hardest hits. All the answers already exist within you. It is your choice to ignite them. Are you ready?

INTRODUCTION

A fictional frog's questions sparked my curiosity as a child. Since this book begins in my childhood, Kermit the Frog (and his maker, Jim Henson) deserve some upfront recognition. Kermit was (is) my favorite puppet. At an early age, his character offered me hope through chaos and safety in dreaming. Kermit never promised certainty and understood that life will always hand you clingy people, chaos, and loud, annoying drummers beating out their emotions. Although he got frustrated at times, he remained empathetic to others. This character's early influence did well to help me develop a habit of introspection and appreciation for humor through chaos.

When stressed, Kermit adjusted his spirit by going back to the pond where he was born to contemplate life and connect with himself. My vision of Kermit's character is empathetic, humorous, and questioning. These are some of the qualities we can learn to develop as persevering skills through daily upsets and long-term adversity. Kermit continued to explore the meaning behind things with patience and curiosity. He didn't expect to have all his prayers answered, and neither should we.

In this book, I go back to the time I was raised to reflect and refocus on my life's most simple and precious gifts. These gifts are the people who helped me piece together a strong and successful life path. I credit many people, my toughest trials, and my commitment to faith, self-love, and gratitude for lessons learned in becoming a stronger adult.

To contemplate on the wisdom you've gathered over a lifetime ignites new questions and understanding about yourself. When you are more introspective, you build a powerful strength to be self-inspired. Although we are not in competition with others, when you are self-inspired to live with more depth and vitality, you succeed at levels beyond most people. This book helps you to persevere to succeed beyond uncertainty. It is empowering to know you are fit to handle any chaos that comes your way.

What You Will Gather from This Book

This book answers the question: "How can I succeed when I am faced with so much responsibility and uncertainty?"

All of us need to learn how to persevere well in order to succeed personally and professionally through adversity. The three-decade inspirational evolution of my personal experience has been filled with hardship and success. Imagine those major points of uncertainty, fear, doubt, and disappointment in your life. How do you handle them? Could the way you handle them be why you are so stressed?

I believe you've already persevered through a great deal. I also believe you're frustrated with all the stress, doubt, and exhaustion that never seem to end. The key here is to help you persist and succeed by no longer sacrificing your health in the process.

My inner purpose is to help you develop a more aware, mindful, and connected relationship with yourself so that you can be:

- Less disappointed in the face of uncertainty;
- More confident in the face of self-doubt;
- Less fearful of taking the next step in life.

To help you achieve the highest level of commitment to yourself, you must:

- Take advantage of a self-care contract that keeps you accountable to this process;
- Return to your self-commitment contract often.

I am not here to manage your stress. I believe you manage enough things. I am here to help you explore your stress response in relation to what I'm calling the Fiery Four Devils behind stress:

1. Uncertainty
2. Fear
3. Doubt
4. Disappointment

Exercise Advantage

You don't have to dread exercising. What you'll find in this book are exercises that challenge your relationship with the Fiery Four Devils behind stress. These exercises work to inspire you to take simple, proactive, and effective action in your life. This leads to a more peaceful, less stressful, successful life.

Enjoy simple and practical steps to success. Choose to engage with one, two, or all of these exercises until you feel you've mastered effective daily habits for yourself. Then, keep practicing these over your lifetime.

As a first-time published author, I wish to connect us through personal stories of major hardship, stress, mindset challenges, resilience, and persistence. This is not a book about stress management techniques you can find in a Google search. I'm not here to bore you with the latest statistics on how bad stress is for you. This is about personal development, improving your relationships, and building peace and harmony into any or every part of your life.

To Help You Succeed

I offer practical methods for thriving in your daily life. As I've come to learn, it truly is attention to your inner world that creates profound and lasting progress, and it is simpler than it sounds. Simple is where happy is found!

You no longer have to worry about finding time, searching for a life purpose to be happy, or waiting to catch a break so you can fulfill a hobby or dream. Seek to honor first what's inside of you and work to create a more meaningful journey of contribution. Keeping track of a simple weekly vision is all you need in order to feel progress.

What You Will Gain

- Real-life stories to inspire hope and movement through uncertainty;
- Access to a visual diagram to trigger daily, weekly, monthly, and yearly habits and progress to develop your strength and success through uncertainty;
- Pyramid of Perseverance: Proactive Levels of Success™
- Life Performance Awareness Model™

Bonus

If you would like your FREE Proactive Planning Companion to this book email me at amy@amymccann.com subject line 'PPC Please.' This guide pulls together everything you explore in these chapters.

Ignite a Practical Daily Purpose to Feel More Alive

Do you feel a pressure from self-help gurus to find a life purpose? We're told this is where we will achieve the highest degree of personal fulfillment. How can we get there when we're busy fighting to manage daily stress? You've probably heard lots of people say that finding and following your passion is where happiness lives. This feels unreachable when daily life is stressed. You might worry. What if I never reach the point of finding a greater life purpose or passion in life? This type of uncertainty is a very real fear for a lot of people. Is this a fear of yours? If so, you will be relieved to know we will focus your energy on a practical daily purpose

I recently learned something profound about purpose and passion from a woman I admire. She is in her eighth decade of life. To me, she has become a master at connecting to a daily life purpose. I believe many of us take for granted what's in front of us. We might stick to an anxious search to find purpose somewhere out there and forget to attend to the simple things first. This woman is steadily attending to purpose that changes daily. This sparks newness in her life and expands her personal growth.

One day this inspiring woman and I were chatting over tea. I asked, "What do you think when it comes to finding a life purpose?" While stirring her tea she answered, "I don't believe we find a life purpose. I believe it either finds us, or it's up to us to doing something that serves a good purpose. I believe my purpose has always been to keep learning. I meet people my age who are stubborn and think they have life figured out. I think stubbornness is the same as being dead. I think learning something new every day is a purpose that makes me feel alive."

She went on to tell me that every day she asks what her purpose is for the day. Then, she sets about doing her housework. At some point an answer arrives and is different from day to day. She said, “Sometimes my purpose is to sharpen my mind, so I can play a better game of scrabble with my neighbor. My job after lunch is to learn some new words. Most of the time I ask, ‘How can I help someone today and make their day better?’ Isn’t that a good purpose? If the answer is to bake a pie for my neighbor and I’m out of sugar, then my purpose is to get off my duff, get dressed, call my ride, and go buy some sugar! I don’t like to wait to do things. If I have a purpose to get something done, I get it done.”

When it comes to finding something you’re passionate about I learned something else from this woman. In this same conversation about purpose I asked, “What would you say to someone who feels they have to find a passion to be happy? With a smile she said, “I didn’t always find passion in my marriage and I was married for over fifty years. It didn’t mean I wasn’t happy. I would say passion comes from learning. Don’t be like some of the people my age who act like they’re dead already.”

You will engage in a practical daily purpose to build strengths in perseverance. This is the path to clearing your mind. When your mind is clear you can begin to act to discover who it is you wish to be on a daily basis. When you get excited about who you are and all you are capable of you begin to have more moments of passionate feeling about life. If you can remember that success isn’t about feeling passionate and happy all the time, you’ll be in healthy connection with all that life has to offer. This is about participating in your life, not waiting for the right time to feel more fulfilled.

A connection back to self allows for exploration. Let's make a life-lasting commitment to ignite a daily practical plan that feels purposeful beyond a daily checklist.

This plan prepares you to think more clearly about your greater life purpose. It is a practical and steady purpose to build your strength. Otherwise, how could you possibly have the energy to focus on a greater vision or purpose to contribute in the world?

Create a Meaningful Next Chapter

"Life isn't about finding yourself, it's about creating yourself."

~George Bernard Shaw

Why are so many of us on a quest to find ourselves? Where did we get lost, and what's the guarantee we will ever find ourselves?

If you feel you've lost yourself in the process of disappointing setbacks, it's difficult to imagine creating a meaningful next chapter in your life. How can anyone flow forward through disappointment when the mind is busy searching? Anytime I feel lost, I imagine myself shifting out of lost gear into creative gear. Learning to visualize is a powerful skill. If you find it difficult to visualize, you can choose to speak, record, or write out the changes you wish to see.

Once the personal search for yourself has been called off, you are automatically in a position to think creatively. You'll no longer feel exhausted because your mind has been cleared and reprogrammed to think differently.

Creating yourself into the new person you wish to become is an energizing process. You will know you are growing when there is some discomfort attached to your efforts. Imagine yourself cutting the weeds of disappointment. At the same time, you can choose to close down the belief that you are lost. You can choose to quiet the mind of its busy search to find itself. Instead of telling yourself you feel lost, tell yourself you are a creator and master of your mind. Small mindset shifts create magnificent power in moving you out of the vines of disappointment and into the arms of creative harmony.

Take Time to Pause

I would like to pause to say that I do hope today finds you well and that you'll feel fully alive as you turn the pages of each chapter. However, there's a chance you may be having a difficult day.

You might think you should just push through each chapter, no matter how you feel. After all, isn't that what perseverance is? Actually, no, it isn't. To persevere well is to remain steady in the face of obstacles. One way to achieve success in perseverance is to keep in steady connection to your self-care. Self-care leads to clearer thinking and problem solving. Your first test in healthy perseverance is to learn to step away rather than push through as your first option.

I do wish to recognize that you might feel whatever you are going through is an emergent life-or-death circumstance. Divorce, death of a loved one, job loss—these can all bring about fears that we just may die in response. When we are fearful, we step into a survival reaction. You might want to rush to save yourself or be saved by someone or a book. The good news is that very few life circumstances or events are actual emergencies that require you to be saved. Work to be healthy, and the feeling that you might die dissipates.

In case your mind is heavy in clouds today and you are having a hard time concentrating, trying to engage with the exercises in this book might not be an effective activity. It's not effective to try to remove old habits when you're stuck in them. I would like to suggest that it is best to come back when you're more rested than you might feel right now.

The advice to pause was given to me by a counselor I was meeting with years ago. I was in the habit of calling him only when a personal crisis hit. This left me a curled-up mess. Imagine me crunched in the corner of an overstuffed chair. Tissues were flying, and my body felt stuck on the runway of life. I was a hot mess ready to spontaneously combust. It's no wonder the counselor was not easily able to extinguish my fiery display of madness.

When I spoke, fear crackled through my voice like burning logs in a fireplace. Doubt about my future crushed my chest like a vine. Disappointment surged through my veins. The feelings of uncertainty fired off in unison with my limbic brain. I was basically engaging in a very expensive fireworks display of emotion. The moment I began scheduling counseling sessions on days I was better rested, I made progress.

Although I'm not a professional counselor or therapist, I seek to help you make progress as well. We will focus on moving you forward. We will take a few meaningful steps backward just to uncover some important gifts you've collected along your life's journey. You'll no doubt love the process of growth you'll experience without the need for an overstuffed chair to comfort you. When you're stressed, you can't think straight. When you're clear, peace is near.

My Stories Could Help You

"Amy is a real person who has had real challenges and overcame them. Amy's personal story is very compelling and touches on many aspects that most people can relate to."

~Marie Drake

The indelible space and times I share with you are my first introductions to all things frightening— stress, fear, uncertainty, doubt, and disappointment. These became my personal devils for a long time after I allowed them to disrupt me.

It wasn't until I learned to form better relationships with these feelings that I could live with more inner peace. My stories could help you view your life more optimistically, and with greater energy to face and embrace struggles. If you feel like you're in a rut it helps to connect to inspiring stories to remind yourself, you're not alone. You will feel supported, challenged, and relieved of emotional upset along the way.

My stories help you to break free of any lingering emotional attachments you may have to negative events or people. You can rest assured that a balanced life is possible. All it takes is some attention to some inner strengths. All of this can be accessed and practiced today. In the end you will be a more graceful, clear thinking person. You'll no longer feel paralyzed in the face of disappointment because you'll be secure in your ability to handle tough situations.

I will help you think like a beginner so that your mind is open to new ways of thinking and problem solving. You'll learn how to navigate anxious feelings of resentment and jealousy that can squash your confidence. Anytime I lose my connection to a beginner's mind, internal chaos erupts. A closed, chaotic mindset crushes new opportunities to expand. This is where stress rears its ugly head.

What I Learned from Others Could Move You

This book is grounded in honoring the people (and characters) who taught me the very wisdom and lessons that will help you live with more depth and vitality. It is about lessons in the most burning and paralyzing situations. It's about expansion of your personal universe, to which I refer as your spirit. Spirit here means your breath, character, energy, and attitude. Exploring these is your open door to a better life ahead.

We will walk together through the good, bad, and ugly things that those I've loved have suffered. What I learned from these people was this:

- The courage to persevere isn't an automatic gift you receive when you go through something bad;
- Imagination can be used for intelligent stress reduction;
- Strength is a word that lives on the other side of survival.

Proactive Measures of Success

It will soon make sense to start living a more proactive life that enriches your life today. To be proactive means to take care prior to the next appearance of the Fiery Four Devils we refer to as uncertainty, doubt, disappointment, and fear.

In the meantime, you can get excited about this: Each exercise in this book is renewable. This means each is adaptable over time at every stage of life and will serve to help when the smelly stuff hits the fan. You will have the opportunity to easily navigate a combination of learning styles that connect to your creative and analytical mind.

With all of this in mind, you'll enjoy stopping points along the way that allow you to drink in your progress and attend immediately to your body, mind, and spirit. Soon, the Fiery Four Devils will be less likely to burn you as you learn to address your relationship with each.

PART I: UNCERTAINTY STRIKES

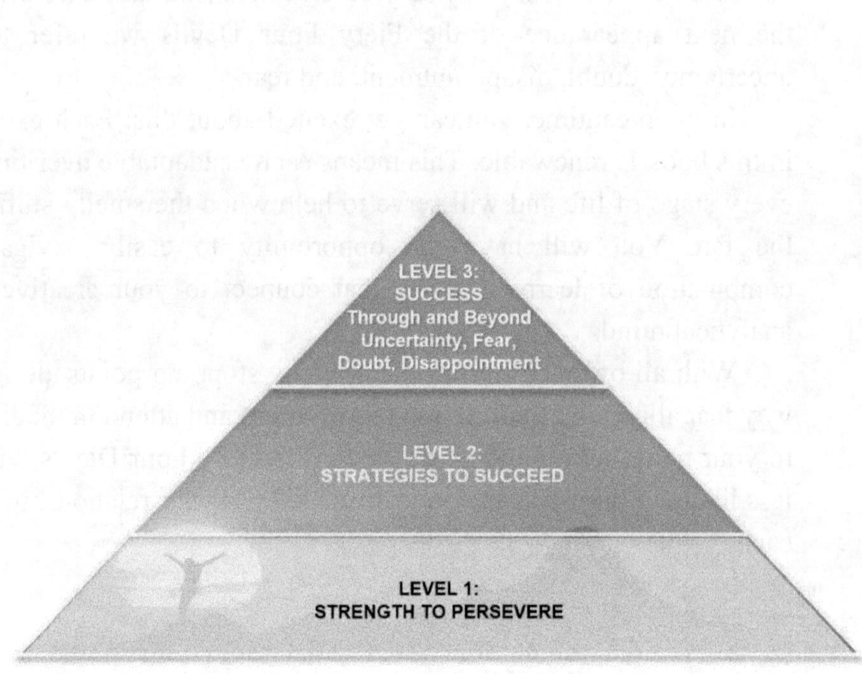

CHAPTER 1
EARLY BURNING LESSONS IN STRESS

A Fiery Story of Uncertainty

My eyes blinked rapidly in an effort to clear away tears. Balancing on my toes, my body was stuck between the waistlines and elbows of relatives. I was eight years old and in no mood for being ignored. It was a struggle to see what was happening on the other side of the neighbor's kitchen window.

In the moments to come, I would catch sight of an image that would leave an indelible mark in my memory. No amount of blinking could ever erase what I was about to witness. It wasn't Halloween. Still, the unfolding scenes would suggest we were most definitely part of something scary.

I tugged hard on my grandmother's nightgown, perhaps in an effort to wake myself from this chaos. Standing just eleven inches above four feet, my grandmother, Nona, as we called her, seemed tall to me. She didn't need to stand on her toes like I did. With her feet flat on the ground, she held a white-knuckled grip to the back of kitchen chair.

Then, as any wacky dream would have it, I must have landed in an episode of *Bugs Bunny*. I could swear I heard Porky Pig's character say, "Th-th-th-that's all folks" as my Nona lost grip of the chair and fell straight to the floor with a thud. To my surprise, a few giggles bubbled up. Maybe this was all a dream? This thought brought some comfort.

Through the chaos, someone must have moved Nona to the nearby couch in the adjacent living room. Her right arm was draped over a neatly folded facecloth stretched across her forehead.

Now that I knew Nona was okay, my eyes went back to the window. I could see my uncle approaching the house. His head drooped, and he clutched a towel that was wrapped around his hand. The neighbor gasped and quickly covered her mouth with her hand. This gave a clue that a real-life nightmare was unfolding.

Moments Before

Before things got scary, it was magical how I arrived at the window in the first place. As if she had turned into a bird, my sister Pam must have sprouted wings to be able to fly her two little sisters and two younger cousins down our farmhouse staircase. How was she able to do this with a broken leg? In my mind, she proved once again that she had special powers.

Growing up, I couldn't wait to be around my sister to see what kinds of magic she had up her sleeve. Her mysterious, imaginative stories kept me in awe of what was possible. To me, a flight down the staircase could have been her next natural power. Still, I had no idea why we had been flown in the first place.

Just moments before our flight down the stairs, we were happily rehearsing a puppet show. I insisted I star as the voice of Kermit the Frog. Our giggles echoed through the house as we each took turns trying on silly voices. This show was scheduled to be the morning entertainment for our parents. We had no idea our giggles would be rudely interrupted and that the show would never come to be.

A loud crackling sound caught my attention. More fireworks? It was July 5, 1981, just one day following Independence Day here in the United States. It was possible that these noises were fireworks. Suddenly, Kermit flew straight out of my hand and clear across the room as a loud boom shook the house. I remembered learning about sonic booms in school and wondered if that's what this was. In any case, it made four little girls jump.

A woman's scream made its way through the floor vent in my bedroom. It was my aunt, and this made my cousins nervous. We would soon learn that the crackling sounds were not in celebration of independence. This had not been a sonic boom either. The sound that caused Kermit to leap from my hands would mark a moment of dependence on others to help support our family.

The Nightmare Is Clear

Back at the neighbor's window, a burning sensation bubbled in the pit of my stomach. I began to piece together what was happening, and fear was blooming. I felt a lump the size of a grape growing in my throat, which made it difficult to swallow. It turns out this would be nothing compared to the black smoke that would arise to suffocate any lingering hope that this was all a dream.

I made my escape out the front door. As I reached the edge of the neighbor's driveway, my legs froze. Why were my feet suddenly glued to the pavement? I could see bright flames dancing on the side of the house. My eyes played tricks. It was no dance. It looked like a devil licking the side of our house. With each lap of his tongue, the devil roared loudly.

My knees jiggled, and I imagine I must have looked a bit like the shaky tin man from *The Wizard of Oz*. It was an odd sensation turning into a Jell-O-like statue. I wanted to scream, but no sound came out of my throat. Clutching my nightgown, I feared the worst. Oliver! Where was Oliver, our dog? Where was Pierre? Pierre was our cat. Did anyone remember to save our two guinea pigs, Fernando and Jessica? Were they still stuck in their cage?

Where were all my pets? A moment of hope arose. Maybe my sister flew them out of the house like she did us? Yes, this must have been what happened. Maybe they were safe inside the neighbor's shed and I just couldn't see them. I couldn't bear the thought of the animals being trapped in the devil's mouth.

My mind tortured me: What about all the stuffed animals? Were they trapped under the puppet stage? Where did Kermit land when he flew out of my hands and across the room? Where was my bright blue journal? I wanted to run in and save it all. Still, I couldn't move, let alone run. Where was the oil to get my legs moving?!

My thoughts were interrupted when once again my body was swooped up. This time, it was my neighbor throwing me over his shoulder. This wasn't as fun a ride as flying down the staircase.

At the window once again, I could see a figure that looked like an unwrapped mummy with arms stretched out like a scarecrow.

Surely, my eyes were playing tricks on me again. This couldn't be my brother. No, it was too scary a thought. To my horror, my eyes were telling the truth. What looked like bandages was in fact skin, draping off of my fifteen-year-old brother's body. The devil, it seemed, had swallowed him and spit him out.

At eight years old, fear and uncertainty had been firmly planted in me. I would learn that my brother Doug had suffered third-degree burns over 90% of his body. He was as a victim of the house fire. We would also come to see that he was anything but a victim of life.

Hope Ignites

"Maybe it is God's way of bringing our family together." This was the answer my sister Pam gave when I asked, "Why did this happen to our family?" It was hours since I first saw the devil's tongue lapping at our house and the image of my brother looking like an unwrapped mummy. Pam had set up camp for her two little sisters and cousins in the neighbor's den. As she lay beside me, stroking my hair, I accepted her answer. Pam's gift to me was this:

hope and possibility that maybe our situation wasn't so grim after all. It was a hopeful influence on how I would handle future traumas and uncertainty.

Our neighbor peeked her head through the door of the den. She explained that my uncle had been my brother's hero that day. It made sense now. His hand had been wrapped in a kitchen towel to cover the burn he suffered while saving my brother's life.

The neighbor's house grew still. I missed my uncle's famously contagious laughter. It was an eerie feeling to see him so silent. His hand was now wrapped in a bandage rather than a towel. As the neighbor moved away, my uncle peeked in to whisper good night to his girls and nieces and blew us kisses. The light from the kitchen changed his skin tone. Instead of brown, he seemed to have turned a paler gray color. I lay my head on my pillow contemplating all that had happened that day. I considered what my sister said and prayed like I had never prayed before that my brother would live.

Burning Story Reflection

Has the story from my past moved you in some way? Although our stories may be very different, you and I are familiar with the kinds of stress and pain that erupt when life hits hard. It's especially difficult when it hits without warning. While this first story is extreme, it illustrates all the burning flames we might experience on any given day. These are what we will address in this book.

When bad things happen, we can feel a sense of doom. Everyday life can feel just as dramatic when we aren't handling our fears well. Stress can become an ongoing weekly theme that can invite feelings of hopelessness.

When it comes to stress management, how many books and articles have you read that focus on sleep, healthy diet, meditation, gratitude journaling, and exercise? These are, in fact stress reducers for the mind, body, and spirit. These are scientifically proven to improve mood and happiness, so what's so wrong that most of us can't or won't do these things?

My opinion on the topic of stress is that we're not focused enough as a society on the behind-the-scenes reasons we're stressed in the first place. Sure, most of us are quick to blame our stress on the most obvious factors: jobs, kids, and financial responsibilities. But are these to blame for why we're snapping at our kids, not able to get a good night's sleep, and wanting to crawl in a hole some days?

Could it be internal factors driving our behaviors? Are we mostly fearful, disappointed, or doubtful of ourselves or uncertain about where we're headed? If these internal stressors are driving us, why are we busy blaming everyone and everything else for our misery?

Here are some real-life internal stressors posted by some of my coaching group students:

> **Fear:** I'm afraid I can't step away from my responsibilities because my family wouldn't do well without my attention.
>
> **Doubt:** I doubt anyone will notice how hard I work unless I keep pushing.
>
> **Uncertainty:** I don't know what my wife would say if I wasn't working as hard as I am now. She might worry that we don't have enough money.
>
> **Disappointment:** I'm never getting into another relationship. I've been disappointed too many times to trust anyone ever again.

When it comes to stress, it pays to know what's really bothering you behind the scenes of your job, relationship with your family, and your finances. It sounds specific to say my job is killing me. Is it the actual job itself that's killing you? If so, the question to ask is why do you stay?

Could it be a disappointment in yourself that keeps you from leaving this job you feel is weighing down your energy? What type of fear could be burning in your mind that tells you worse things might happen if you took a new direction? Do well to be as specific and simple as possible in every area of life. If negative stress is mostly how you experience your life, get down to the fiery reasons behind why you do what you do, say what you say, and react how you react. This is where you gain clarity to move ahead, even in the face of uncertainty.

Fiery Four Devils and Burnout

"Energy and persistence conquer all things."

~ Benjamin Franklin

Who can sleep when uncertainty is the major player in your marriage? How can you think to eat a carrot over a chip when the trail of crumbs has worked to soothe your disappointment? A walk might be out of the question when fear of being seen in a vulnerable state has you glued to the couch. This is the work of one or more of the fiery players to which we refer as the devils behind stress.

I believe we're too busy living between the flames of uncertainty, fear, doubt, and disappointment throughout any single day. These are the things that wear us down or burn us out. If you want more energy, you need to ignite some new habits of perseverance that reprogram or extinguish these flames.

This energy you will generate comes from your awareness of your stress response and your relationship with the fiery four devils in all areas of your life. When you learn to master these, you'll be more fit to handle things daily. You'll be more confident to face any big obstacle life decides to throw at you, such as a house fire, disability, divorce, and death.

Here are a few ways you can gain energy:

- ☐ Commit to work to extinguish paralyzing self-doubt.
- ☐ Choose to fuel your excitement with dramatic change instead of getting fired up by drama.
- ☐ Choose to build a better relationship with uncertainty, fear, doubt, and disappointment.

With more energy, you'll be better able to press on without a guaranteed risk of burning down in the process. I consider this to be healthy perseverance.

Beat Stress in the Face of Uncertainty: Ignite Kindness

If only life were nicer to us, kinder to us, more giving to us, we'd have more time to take care of ourselves. Right? It's easy to get caught up in the feeling that we've been dealt bad cards or that our families and the world owe us something. This sets us up to respond to rather than participate in life.

The less you participate in your relationship with stress, the more it will work to burn you. Waiting for life to be kinder to you is a ticket to victimhood and isolation. Both of these can lead to unnecessary emotional stress. Why not work to be kinder to yourself?

There was a time in my life when I was overly optimistic in waiting for professional home health organizations to provide in-home care that I temporarily lost focus on myself. In waiting for the solution, I wasn't doing myself any favors in the present. I became a responder and was no longer participating in my self-care to the optimal level. Then, bitterness and a need to control things set in.

How often have you caught yourself waiting on others to fix the situation? Have you gotten stuck waiting on permission to take a break? Isn't it tiring waiting for your wife, your husband, your boss, or your friend to change so you'll feel happier? If so, I believe today might be your day to be kinder to yourself. Imagine your relief when you know that no matter what happens, you have the power to create a beautiful, successful life. If you're not dealing with your disappointments, you are not being kind to yourself. How can you expect to be a personal success if you're busy responding to or waiting on others?

Aside from the consequences of waiting on others, we allow our complaining friends to wear us down. It could be that we settle into the belief that a good friend is one who listens to complaints, so we do our best to open our ears to their miseries. Is this the kindest we can be to ourselves and our friends? Let's work to empower ourselves to engage in constructive conversations that create movement. What if we weren't afraid to find new friends who are moving in the direction of calm instead of reactive? These are some ways we could choose to be kinder to ourselves.

Extinguish Your Survival Lifestyle

What do you say when someone asks, "How did your week go?" Do you often use the words "I survived" to answer the question?

A feeling that you've survived a week can feel exhilarating if you've succeeded in staying strong through a tough challenge. You made it, and congratulations! However, disappointment can become your devil if you feel you're surviving each and every week. Fatigue can accompany disappointment and can lead to burnout. Here's a quick way to see if you might be on a survival lifestyle track.

Are You A Weekly Survivor?
Here's a Quick Way to Check-in

✎Someone asks, "How did your week go?"
Most often, I answer, "I survived!"

Possible Symptoms of Stress Associated: Fatigue, Exhaustion, Burnout
Possible words I might say: "I can barely hold my head up some days."

~

✎I complain to friends about all that went wrong in your week more often than celebrating my small achievements.

Possible Emotions Associated: Frustration, Anxiety
Possible words I might say: "Once again, look what happens to me."

~

✎More often than not, I feel uncertain where my week is headed (or I feel certain it is headed in a bad direction).

Possible Mental Stress Associated: Inability to think clearly
Possible words you might say: "I have no idea when I'll catch a break"

Amy McCann Coaching™

I believe it is a severely energy-sapping goal to strive to survive your life day by day. Living a maxed-out, stressed-out lifestyle could eventually cost you your health.

I think you and I can do a lot better. I know it is possible to have more time than you think to do things you want to do. I know it is possible to run a company, raise children well, spend quality time with loved ones, and still have time for your hobbies. This isn't just talk or hopeful thinking. This isn't about perfection. It's about healthy perseverance into and through obstacles we face every day.

If a TGIF lifestyle feels like survival, could it be time to retire this way of living in favor of more peace? If so, let's flow forward with an open mind to new beginnings no matter what you might face tomorrow.

CHAPTER 2
STRENGTHS IN PERSEVERANCE

Inner Strengths Defined

I bring you some definitions of strengths that I believe are central in your quest to succeed through uncertainty. I will help you connect to and exercise these strengths in a simple outline later in this book.

We will explore how to ignite the following strengths in perseverance and success:

- Emotional Strength
- Mindset Strength
- Survival Strength
- Spiritual Strength
- Strength to Make Choices
- Strength to Be Less Perfect
- Daily Strength to Persist

Ignite Emotional Strength

When you think of an emotionally strong person, how do you see him or her? You might imagine him or her facing obstacles no matter how difficult. You might see those obstacles as big or overwhelming. You might envision someone soldiering on through hardship. You may even wonder, "How do they do it?"

That vision of a strong person is how I was living my life and how many people claimed they saw me. People often asked, "How do you do it?" For a long time, I felt annoyed at this question. I didn't know how to answer it until I realized its value.

A woman once said that I was a role model of strength, meaning that I seemed to persevere through anything. I'll share the story behind her perception later. Because of others' curiosity about how I might be doing things, I learned that there is a healthy way to persevere and an unhealthy way.

At first, I persevered the healthy way. I was clear minded, grateful, and emotionally, spiritually, and physically grounded. This is because I was practicing daily meditation, gratitude, and physical exercise and was connected to my emotional health. These habits were all born from my professional training as a stage actress as well as my attention to self-development practices.

For a long time, I was able to make it through fear, doubt, disappointment and uncertainty with confidence. Then, my confidence seemed to disappear overnight. So, what went wrong? I allowed the devil of disappointment to rule my circumstance and extinguish my healthy habits. As my mindset went up in flames, I was left to rifle through the ashes of self-doubt.

To become strong again, I needed to regroup and reprogram. I had to reignite a simple practice to think like a beginner—to begin with fresh intent to remove any weight of assumption I may have adopted regarding my situation. A beginner's mind invites open thinking. We will go through the process of developing your beginner's mind in a later chapter. This will extinguish any frozen thoughts you might have about yourself or your situation.

Ignite Physical Strength

Physical strength here refers to your physiological awareness. It isn't about how much weight you can lift in a gym. This is about strategy. Recently, my husband Sean took down a man twice his size in a Brazilian Jiu Jitsu competition. Although my husband is muscular, it was his attention to strategy and technique that mattered and is why he has won many gold medals.

One winning strategy when it comes to improving your physical strength is to stay in regular tune with how your body is speaking to you. When you are feeling uncertain, does your back ache? Where doubt is concerned, do you find you experience more headaches? If you're feeling afraid where in the body do you feel stressed? When someone disappoints you is there tension in your shoulders? Being aware of how often these types of physical stress show up this helps you narrow down which devil you need to extinguish. Your body is only as strong as your willingness to keep it tuned. Physical awareness is a gold standard in personal development.

I provide you with a physical strength check-in exercise that will simply help you:

- Journal any aches and pains you may have caused by stress associated with uncertainty, fear, doubt, and disappointment.
- Set an easy habit in self-care.

Ignite a Proactive Path of Personal Success

In my approach to stress reduction, I have designed methods that are proactive and intended to ignite personal success in any area of life. I will take you through a journey of helping you unwrap some of the inner gifts you possess and that others have passed on to you. Your inner awareness and connection will help you better move through times of uncertainty.

In order to feel a higher level of success and a lower level of stress, you must learn to persevere well. This means moving beyond a survival mindset when it comes to your daily life. Many of us can push through life, and I believe this can fool us into a false sense of success. Don't let this happen to you.

Ignite Mindset Strength

If you are sick of this self-help topic, I will say that I don't believe enough can be said of the power of your mind to help you face the devil of uncertainty.

To ignite a strong mind is to:

- Choose to become a kind of mental warrior against the negative upsets that crop up in your daily life.
- Be proactive in daily mindset.

By a strong mind, I mean:

- The willingness to see things as a beginner to ignite new ways to problem solve when things go wrong.
- The ability to pause or slow down long enough to freeze emotion in order to see things objectively.

A Fighting Mindset is Stressful

Think of a time someone announced not getting the kind of service he or she felt was "deserved." Chances are this person fought to seek out justice while engaging in a blame game. Situations we view as unfair can ignite a fighting mindset and a fighting response. The question is, how often? Could disappointment be your devil behind your fight response? If so, this devil may shout, "Hey world, you owe me!"

To extinguish a fighting mindset means taking a deep breath first. If you can't remember to take a breath, it simply means you need a bit more practice. Snap on your beginner's intelligence and work to light more graceful habits in communicating your disappointment.

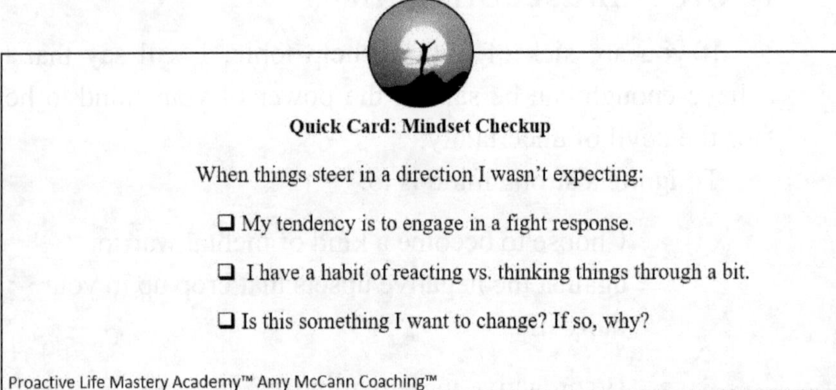

Quick Card: Mindset Checkup

When things steer in a direction I wasn't expecting:

- ❑ My tendency is to engage in a fight response.
- ❑ I have a habit of reacting vs. thinking things through a bit.
- ❑ Is this something I want to change? If so, why?

Proactive Life Mastery Academy™ Amy McCann Coaching™

Putting Your Mind to Work

The smell of leather mixed with my mother's famous spaghetti sauce as she placed three blue boxes at my feet. Each box contained one piece of a leather luggage tag—the tag, the strap, and the buckle. It was the winter I turned fourteen, and I was set to work from home piecing together thousands of luggage tags. My mother brought these tags home from the factory where she worked.

"Why would you want to do a boring job like that?" my friends asked. All I could see were the benefits:

> I would get to work at home by the comfy fireplace.
>
> I would get to watch my favorite TV shows while I worked.

> I would get to earn some money for the next summer without leaving the house.

I took one last sip of my hot cocoa out of a straw and got to work stuffing name tags and looping and buckling straps. It was a satisfying exercise of the hands. Perhaps these tags are still in existence, traveling the world. My positive approach to this job is an example of beginner's thinking. I wasn't fixed on how boring it might be. I wasn't only thinking it might help me earn money.

Everyday life is a bit like tedious piece work, isn't it? We're tested each day to fulfill tasks we might find mundane or repetitive. The pain of the mundane tasks throughout the day can weigh us down. You know right away when one task has been ignored and usually regret it later. If you haven't a way to delegate some things, you might beat yourself up for not completing them. To avoid the pain of procrastination, see my next tip.

Tip to Overcome the Pain of the Mundane

A change in mindset acts beyond thinking. If you think tasks are boring you're less likely to attend to them. If you dislike doing laundry for example, consider completing this task as a practice in patience vs. a mundane duty. An ability to be patient doing the things you least enjoy will influence your mindset to get things done and to stop procrastinating. A practice in patience doing mundane tasks are likely to spill over into more meaningful areas of life — relationships — which deserve a high level of patience. The ability to be patient by the way, is a persevering quality — a quality family members will appreciate!

PRACTICAL DAILY MINDSET PRACTICE

Purpose

Set a peaceful mindset to lower stress.

Objective

Effectively improve mood and communication in relationships and/or business.

I've met a lot of people who say they don't have time to mediate. Others feel they would never be able to sit still long enough to calm the mind. If you find it difficult to slow down your mind, here's a quick and simple way to effectively ignite peace into your day.

Instead of worrying the morning away, follow this simple three-step daily mindset practice idea you can do in your mind while brushing your teeth:

> **Appreciate**
> Student Example: Today I choose to appreciate my wife.
>
> **Contemplate**
> Student Example: How can I help make my wife's day be better today than it was yesterday?
>
> **Initiate**
> Student Example: When I am done brushing my teeth, I will appreciate my wife by telling her how much all she's done to show support for my new business means to me.

Tip

Put the words "appreciate," "contemplate," and "initiate" on 3x5 index cards and create them as your own. Put them somewhere you will see them first thing in the morning until this becomes a regular mindset habit. It's old school, but it works!

Sometimes, all it takes is three simple words to put you in a more confident flow and response to life. Simple and effective are what we're after.

Develop Strength in Communication

It feels great to complain! Isn't that why we do it? The question is, does it fit into our journey to persevere and succeed through uncertainty? Also, does it work to improve our relationships? All of the exercises in this book will help you improve communication with yourself so that you may better interact with others. Relationships will improve as a result of your decision to connect with yourself. Here, I share a quick way to develop strength in communication that might come in handy when faced with a complaining friend.

Complaining might feel great at the time, but it also serves to burn out our energy. Lifelong strength in perseverance doesn't run on low batteries. Constructive communication works to steer complaints away and clear the mind for energy in problem solving. This is a mutually beneficial exercise.

Are you ready to ignite strength in communication and your relationships?

YES/AND Positive Approach to Conversations™

Sample Conversation:

Acknowledge a Friend's Problem

"YES, I see you've got a lot on your plate…AND… (tell me more) …"

Activate Positive Emotion

"YES, I've felt that way…AND…I notice you have mustard on your lip (humor)

Accelerate Closure to Conversation

"I hear there's a new scheduling app that might help your situation. I'll be happy to send it…Until next time, you've got this!

This process is inspired by the YES/AND improvisational technique used by actors. The goal in this version is to extinguish complaint, ignite presence, improve listening, and succeed in problem solving.

Amy McCann Coaching™

Survival Strength

I believe you are an expert at surviving. That which has not killed you has worked to make you stronger. Or has it?

I have no doubt you've been through some tough trials. Sometimes survival is the ability to handle a tremendous amount of responsibility on very little sleep. It's those times when you are able to take care of everyone else without collapsing. The problem arises when we stay in survival mode so long that we fool ourselves into thinking this is healthy strength.

How do you know if you've been in survival mode too long, and what do you do to transition into a healthier lifestyle? First of all, don't wait for your body to break down before you realize you've been doing it wrong.

Here's a Quick Perspective

If your daily life is so stressful that a TGIF relief dominates your conversations, it may mean it is time to make some strength shifts from survival expert to perseverance master.

Many of us like the idea of Fridays being the signal for weekend fun or relaxation. You'll know if you've gone too far in survival mode if you are in such a desperate sprint to the finish line to Friday that your body, mind, and spirit are compromised enough to negatively impact your relationships.

Could this you?

I've met students who say they feel out of sorts when they're not busy doing a lot of things. Many mothers I've met admit to believing that large amounts of stress are just part of the experience of being a mother. As a mother of twins, I can say I've had my share of stress. Still, stress doesn't have to rule my day. This is where I challenge you to become comfortable with the idea that stress doesn't have to accompany success. This is where I say be brave to open your mind to new ways of living.

How to Avoid a Long-Term Survival Mindset

- **Don't Fool Yourself:** Just because you're an expert in meeting your responsibilities does not mean that you are healthy in body, mind, and spirit. Be proactive in your health.
- **Set a New Mindset:** Believe that you are not destined or obligated to be stressed.
- **Be Aware:** How are you handling common daily upsets? (Check back in with your most

typical/common stress response over the past weeks or months.)

Pillar of Strength: A Visual Perspective

I feel a bit stressed when someone refers to another person as a pillar of strength. When I visualize myself as a pillar, I see myself holding up a very heavy load. What if my pillar crumbles due to the weight of stress?

This is one way to look at strength differently, anyway. If you are a visual person, imagine yourself as a pillar. The top represents your mind. The worries you carry about work, family life, and confidence in yourself feel heavy, don't they? The middle of your pillar (your spirit) has cracked from the weight of stressful responsibilities or circumstances. When you are busy carrying so much, the base of your pillar (your body) weakens. When your body becomes tired, you aren't as likely to want to move forward.

Being called a pillar of strength might feel like a compliment. At the same time, you might feel exhausted by this position. What if you could rebuild your thought process to think of yourself as a pyramid of strength? Why try so hard to carry the weight of the world? Why stay busy trying to do all this balancing the hard way? What would happen if you could start to care about how you carry and store the thoughts, feelings, and emotions we experience?

It is a day for new beginnings and a day you might wish to retire a pillar of strength status to build a new life as a pyramid of strength.

Spiritual Strength

When I speak about spiritual strength in this book, I am referring to your inner spirit (breath). This book is not about steering you toward any one religion. Here, we connect back to your inner character. It is the one behind the mask that rarely reveals itself because it is stifled by stress.

In this book, your spirit is the breath and attitude you carry when moving through life.

If you are busy being reactive, your breath is labored or shallow. When your breath is compromised, attitudes become strained.

If you are quick to respond instead of pausing, your interactions could be dismissive or explosive.

The point here is to help you be self-inspired to discover or rediscover the kind of inner spiritual strength you possess through breath and attitude. This is what ignites confidence to generate graceful presence in everyday life.

I'm careful not to take for granted the power of connection to spirit to generate peaceful energy. To continue my personal growth, I regularly seek out spiritual teachers and mentors. No matter how you approach spiritual strength, it is a useful and meaningful player in any persevering journey.

Ignite Strength to Make Choices

The fact that you have the freedom to make choices is your power. I don't have to tell you that you can use it for good or ill will. Still, where are you on the spectrum from choosing personal empowerment to blaming others for your fears, doubts, and disappointments?

There is strength in making choices that are empowering to your overall spirit. Still, you need to know if this kind of strength is worth it to you. A quick way to know is to become more aware of the short-term benefits and potential long-term consequences of your choices.

Here's a common choice I see many people making:

A woman calls her ex-husband the biggest idiot loser that ever lived in her Facebook status update.

Short-Term Benefit: she receives an overwhelming supportive response from friends.
Potential Immediate Consequences: her child opens the laptop, innocently sees the post, and comments about her father.

Potential Long-Term Consequence: trust is broken.

Ask Yourself:

- Am I willing to keep making the choices I'm making?
- Are my choices engaging or blaming?
- Do my choices have the potential consequence of hurting my reputation or hurting others?

At the very least, choosing to reflect upon your choices is a strength in itself.

Strength to Be Less Perfect

"Being gritty doesn't mean not showing pain or pretending everything is okay. In fact, when you look at healthy and successful and giving people, they are extraordinarily meta-cognitive. They're able to say things like, 'Dude, I totally lost my temper this morning.' That ability to reflect on yourself is signature to grit."

~Angela Duckworth

Perseverance is about facing obstacles, not masking them. When you choose to pretend that everything is just fine, you risk self-absorption and lose focus on the issues at hand. Choose to be honest about how you're handling things and you become clear-minded in your ability to move forward.

Some potential benefits of choosing to be less than perfect include:

- Appearing more attractive to your spouse;
- Appearing more genuine to others;
- Your children feeling more relaxed now that they see that you're not so perfect.

I agree with Angela Duckworth, who is a researcher on the topic of grit. I do believe that it's okay to laugh at yourself when you lose your cool once in a while. It is definitely wise to reflect, laugh, and move on to do better more often. I do not believe it is helpful to be apologizing to everyone all day long for outbursts.

Daily Strength to Persist (Without Reacting Negatively)

"Try to look at your weakness and convert it into your strength. That's success."

~Zig Ziglar

Do you hate it when your day is set to go well and something or someone puts a wrench in it? Daily strength doesn't come from praying that nothing goes wrong. Strength can be a decision to be patient when your car breaks down, for example. Imagine being strong enough to endure this kind of common disruption that it doesn't take your whole day down. You might not be thrilled that your schedule went off the rails, but at least you didn't raise your blood pressure in the process.

What would you consider a situational weakness for you as of late? Are you quick to get upset because your kids missed the bus? Could you imagine yourself making just as quick a decision to say that you've missed the bus once or twice yourself? Would that help to lower the stress in the family unit?

If you are quick to stew, you can learn to be quick to review how you might respond to daily interruptions of schedules. Since I choose to be less than perfect, my kids know there's a chance I might blow my stack. Still, they appreciate it when I take a moment to pause and we each figure out what we need to do to move forward more efficiently.

Being honest about how you're reacting to things beyond your control is:

- A first step in respecting yourself.
- Not an exercise in beating yourself up.
- Considerate of others.

If you do find yourself saying, "These things happen. Now what?" then you are so far ahead of most people today. It doesn't make you any better than anyone else, it simply means you're further ahead in becoming a more peaceful person.

A Proactive vs. Reactive Lifestyle

Largely, your path to strength, according to this book, is to build confidence in your ability to handle and enjoy life on a more regular basis. The most effective way to do this is to live a proactive instead of reactive lifestyle.

Proactive and Persevering Habits to Ignite Success

1) **Daily Purpose:** Grace through active gratitude
2) **Weekly Process:** Beginner's mind intelligence for solutions to stress and clear thinking; ability to ignite courage
3) **Monthly Vision** for peace, harmony, and personal success
4) **Yearly Engagement** to celebrate your progress

When you are busy reacting to life, you are in a continuous state of stress and survival. This leaves little energy left over to handle daily life, let alone a bigger catastrophe.

Many stress management books talk about the importance of sleep, a healthy diet, and exercise as ways to feel happier and calmer. I believe we're not inspired or energetic enough to implement these habits because we are living in various levels of uncertainty, fear, doubt, and disappointment throughout each day.

When these factors aren't dealt with, we become mentally exhausted and physically drained. Who can sleep when the devil of uncertainty is staring us in the face? How can we feel motivated to make a change when we fear what others might think of us? When disappointment burns us over and over, how can we feel confident that we can experience relief or joy?

Strengths We Will Continue to Explore

- Emotional
- Mental
- Choice-Driven
- Physical
- Spiritual
- Daily

CHAPTER 3
PREPARE TO PERSEVERE

Unwrapping Gifts from Positive Role Models

A yellow package the size of a shoe box arrived. My slow efforts to slice the clear tape with a knife would have frustrated my family. I was known to unwrap gifts slowly while others yelled, "Get on with it, already!" There is something special to me about intentionally savoring small moments. I still open gifts in slow fashion, and these Zen moments are no longer rattled by others who display their impatience.

Tucked beneath some bubble wrap and newspaper was an unexpected and most thoughtful gift sent by my oldest sister, Lucille. Peering from beneath the unwrapped layers of newspaper was the face of a 1970s vintage Sunshine Family Doll. So many years ago, my little sister Carol and I mourned the loss of this tiny plastic family that perished in the fire. We hoped we might one day unearth these dolls. The mommy, daddy, and baby dolls lived quite an active life thanks to hours of imaginary play in our handmade doll house gifted by a neighbor.

It was a perfect first birthday gift to my twin daughters. Lucille is my most cherished sister when it comes to creating treasured moments like this one. She took care to search for the dolls online in an attempt to resurrect happy moments from the past. It is meaningful that she would think to pass on a piece of my childhood to her nieces.

I share this story as an introduction to unwrapping some of the gifts your role models may have passed on. With so much uncertainty in front of you, it's helpful to connect to the gifts that exist inside of you. Sometimes, it really is the simplest things that ignite the spirit within us. These are things you may have forgotten about or never thought of as your good fortune tools in times of hardship or stress.

Unwrapping these gifts does two things:

1. Exercises your inner awareness;
2. Honors those who have had your best interest at heart.

I want to invite you to develop a connection to your own good fortune by exercising your gratitude. This works to initiate grace. When you connect back to your inner spiritual gifts, to which I refer as breaths of influence, you ignite graceful motion through uncertainty. This takes the relief of having to search outside yourself for answers when things get tough.

I share with you the special people in my life who helped me connect and gain new perspective. I'm aware you might be in a position where you feel you've had no positive role models in your life. I want to reassure you that you can learn to pull positively from the negative people who may have wounded you emotionally in some way. Later, I'll share a story to help inspire you to consider this.

I begin with appreciation and gratitude for my oldest sister, Lucille, whose passion for reading helped expose me to deeply influential books at a young age. In my eyes, Lucille was wisest in showing me how to connect to myself through the act of gifting me some of her favorite books. My sister took something as simple as reading and made it into a treasured moment anytime she wrote a personal inscription on the inner page. It was rare to see anyone without a book in our house, so reading quickly became a pleasurable hobby for me. When I was little, my mother sent me to a community program called Library School. I was never disappointed by the lady sitting in front of a bright red curtain. The voices she put to the characters made me lean forward with my chin in my hands.

The books Lucille gifted me helped to:

- Make me feel less alone;
- Generate feelings of good fortune through fear and uncertainty.

Soon, we'll work to unwrap your own inner gifts of wisdom to help you feel less alone and in good vibration and generation of good fortune.

Gift of Perseverance #1: Connection to Struggle

"Painful as it may be, a significant emotional event can be the catalyst for choosing a direction that serves us and those around us more effectively. Look for the learning."

~Louisa May Alcott

March through Anxiety:A Story of Connection to Struggle

Clicking my heels three times beneath my desk wasn't enough to magically beam me back home. I stared blankly at the math test in front of me. At that time, numbers were more intimidating than the bottomless well in my neighbor's back yard. There were stories of ghosts in that well, and on this day, their presence would have been welcome.

I was nine years old, thinly framed, with long brown hair that reached the middle of my back. I was a typically dressed child of the 70s, bell bottoms included. I wore large glasses. My friends were jealous that my teeth were so straight while they had to wear braces.

My school days can be summed up with this copy of a report card my mom kept:

Amy's Report Card

Amy is a happy, cheerful, little girl, and a pleasure to have in class. She is a bit of a social butterfly and has lots of friends. At other times, she is quiet, and attends to her work nicely. Amy is also very concerned about her friends. She is a good listener, with a very big heart. However, I believe this can distract her from completing her assignments. Amy is very intelligent, and has many creative abilities, but she does struggle with math. Amy needs encouragement to stay focused. Once she can learn to do this better, she will do well in all subjects.

Back at my school desk, each number on the math test began to bleed together like they do when I forget to wear my glasses.

Time for an Amy daydream session. My eyes darted away from the numbers and toward the decorated classroom windows. I began to count the twenty-eight apples cut from construction paper, each fastened with perfectly placed pieces of tape. I wondered why we weren't allowed to color our apples the way we wanted. I smiled slightly remembering that when the teacher wasn't looking, I dared to add a leaf to the stem of my apple.

My fingers clutched the edge of my desk in a moment of anxiety as I took notice of the window fingerprints and smudges left behind by rambunctious boys ready for recess—a perfectly obsessive distraction from the greater pain of facing the math test. I imagined erasing these cloudy smears in the same way I would erase the teacher's leftover chalk marks when she turned her back.

My best friend, Susan, laughed hysterically each time I would jump up to wipe the chalkboard clean. She wasn't aware that erasing had become my private way of feeling in control of things that looked messy. Through my quest for neatness, I felt more at ease.

You wouldn't have recognized my quest if you had seen my bedroom at home littered with clothes, books, toys, and an unmade bed. The point is I had figured out one way to erase something that bothered me. It was the only kind of subtraction that felt good. After all, life felt scary after losing my pets and my home and seeing my brother suffer.

In my day-dreamy state, I managed to see past the smudgy fingerprints on the windows. I was mesmerized by the red, yellow, and orange leaves swirling in whirlpool fashion on the cracked pavement outside. Nature was, and is, my medicine. This one medicinal dose of nature proved fleeting. As swiftly as the leaves swirled around outside, my head spun quickly to the loud sound of clapping chalk erasers. My teacher's efforts to capture my attention had worked.

My hands grew clammy at the thought of the dreadful math test she wanted me to finish. This feeling of dread plowed over any embarrassment I felt for being called out in front of my friends. Then, after some time trying to focus, an anxious reality surfaced in my mind.

I imagined myself five hours ahead. I was standing in the damp trailer in which our family was now living. The wind gods blew the pungent scent of burnt remains from our family's farmhouse through the windows and into my bedroom. This smell made my pillow case stink.

Apart from the memory of this one frustrating day in the classroom, most days were spent cherishing our family. In my mind, I could imagine my way beyond the musty, stinky environment.

I imagined my sisters and I were the March girls from Louisa May Alcott's book, *Little Women.* We each had our talents, struggles, and dreams. Connecting to these characters helped me feel less alone through this uncomfortable time of uncertainty.

I have kept the original copy of *Little Women* that my sister Lucille gifted me at the age of ten. Here is her inscription:

Dear Little Sister,

It is my hope that you, like me, will discover a part of yourself within each of the March girls.

With Love,
Lucille

It took one special sister and a generous action to pass on a book to help me feel less alone in my personal struggles related to our family. As a bonus, my sister took me to visit the author's gravesite and the Alcott House in Concord, Massachusetts. Although the author was no longer alive to thank in person, it felt good to honor her in some way.

I cherish my sister for her love of books. Passing them on is one example of her ability to create a treasured memory. She helped to influence an early practice to be introspective, for which I am most grateful.

Childhood Inner Wisdom Unwrapped

A connection to others' struggles through stories can help you feel less anxious and alone.

Gift of Perseverance #2: Perspective

"What really counts in life is the quiet meeting of every difficulty with determination to get out of it all the good there is."

~Helen Keller

Imaginary Changes – A Story of Possibilities

The automatic doors at Shriner's Hospitals for Children in Boston, Massachusetts were a magical delight to witness, at least for two little girls from the far north woods of New Hampshire. At six and eight years old, we were thrilled to play anywhere. It wasn't often we got to be in a big city, and there weren't doors like these back home. Butterflies flew rapidly in my belly as I anticipated seeing our big brother.

Soon, my head spun around, and my eyes locked on a bald-headed little girl. A pink crochet blanket with a green bow wrapped around her chest made it possible to guess this was a girl. It didn't take long to notice that she had no eyes. I had never met a blind person, let alone one without eyes at all. It took only moments to see she had no arms, either.

I thought of a woman named Helen Keller. I remembered the book, *The Story of Helen Keller*, which my oldest sister read to me before bed. It had burned in the fire, but I could still feel the essence of this blind and deaf woman's story.

I stood with mouth dropped open and held my breath as I took in her faceless, armless body. My imagination swirled. It didn't take long for me to think that if Helen Keller could do anything, then this girl could, too! This thought caused my shoulders to drop from tension and ignite curiosity. How would she learn to tie her shoes without arms? The thought fascinated me.

I could see nostrils and a tiny hole where this girl's mouth should have been. Strangely, her skin appeared shiny. Later, I came to witness my brother's burns turn from bright red to glossy scars through the healing process. This would explain the shiny skin.

My imagination gave me hope that all was not lost. Anything was possible—that much I had read. Still, it felt like a swarm of butterflies settled in my belly anytime I imagined seeing my brother. I squeezed my six-year-old sister's hand and caught myself staring a little too long at this little girl in front of me. Somewhere I must have been taught that it's rude to stare, so I forced myself to look away. I pretended to be looking at my feet, even though she was blind and couldn't see where my eyes had landed or shifted. The tall, curvy nurse then whisked her away. The butterflies that had found their way inside my belly now flapped wildly about. It seemed another grape had settled in my throat, which made it hard to swallow. These are the uncertain thoughts that flooded my mind:

> Will Doug have a face?
>
> Is he blind, too?
>
> If he lost his legs, will he be in a wheelchair like this little girl?
>
> Will it be forever?

These questions seemed less scary as I kept remembering Helen Keller. I could imagine all the things the little girl and my brother might still be able to do. An early lesson in perspective helped extinguish some of the fears associated with the unknown aspects of my brother's injury.

Childhood Inner Lesson Reflection

Perspective works to dampen fears of the unknown.

Imaginary obstacles in the form of fear can be reimagined into possibilities. Possibilities ignite hope.

Reflection on Perspective

Has anyone in your life ever given you a perspective, whether through a conversation or a book, that helped you see things less fearfully?

How often do you search for a new perspective to help diminish your fears of the unknown?

Is it your tendency to get stuck in a feeling of fear when facing troubling uncertainty?

What specific perspective can you think of that could help you in the present and serve as a life-lasting gift of comfort?

My Notes on Perspective

Gift of Perseverance #3: Kindness Rules

"You can never do kindness too soon, for you never know how soon it will be too late."
~Ralph Waldo Emerson

Scarred, Not Broken: A Story of Kindness through Pain and Healing

The view of the little girl with the pink blanket vanished as her nurse rounded the corner of the hallway.

Finally, our big brother appeared. He looked like a dressed-up mummy ready for Halloween. His entire body was tightly wrapped in bandages. I could easily recognize his closed-lip grin as he approached us. Inside my head, I was screaming, "Yay! He still has his face!"

A smile was revealed from beneath the bandages. My shoulders dropped in relief as I realized my imagination had been wrong. My brother's lips were moving. He could speak! I could see he still had his arms and his legs. And he could see me, which meant he wasn't blind.

I could see he was carrying two upside-down boxes on his knees. He casually asked, "What ya been up to?" Before we could answer, he handed each of us a Monchichi Monkey Doll. These were the most popular dolls of the day. Here he was, in the most painful situation imaginable, giving his little sisters presents.

My brother is probably unaware of how much this small gesture of kindness eased my worries. A tiny selfless act influenced me to see that we can be kind to others even when we are the ones suffering.

A big heart was revealed in my brother that day. The last of the butterflies in my belly flew away. Any leftover scary thought that thrashed about in my mind had permanently settled down.

Childhood Inner Gift Reflection

Compassion and kindness can ease uncertainty and bring joy to grim situations.

To act to help others when you are experiencing pain is to elevate your compassion.

Compassion Reflection

How has kindness served to help me in the past?

Do I presently view kindness as a tool to ease fears?

Is there someone today who would benefit from an act of kindness from me?

Feel free to pause here and journal some of your thoughts about how you might want to demonstrate kindness or compassion moving forward.

My Notes

CHAPTER 4 POSITIVE CONNECTIONS

Positive Connections to Negative Role Models

"A choice to learn from your personal history is a smart decision. It creates movement and allows for easier breathing. It's not something you have to do alone. Seek to be inspired. Then, seek to find someone you can connect with to discuss and resolve your fears and disappointments."

~Amy McCann

Seek Inspiration

I want to reiterate that it is possible to extract some positive lessons from anyone who may have hurt you in the past. Why would this be important to explore in your life? Why not forget about these negative influences?

Here are three simple reasons you might be inspired to explore how past disappointments caused by others may be affecting you in the present:

1. You might release yourself of some emotional pain;
2. You might gain greater clarity about your reactions;
3. You might gain a better understanding of your present fears.

This is not an exercise in forgiving those who have hurt you. This is about healthy respect for how your past hurts may be tying you down. It's also about what you could do to move forward.

If I were resistant to learning from my past hurts, I might quickly connect to Elizabeth Smart. This is a woman who was kidnapped and tortured for months by a stranger at the age of fifteen.

Elizabeth's experience is a far cry from my own, but this isn't about comparison of struggles, it's about connection. Now an adult, Elizabeth is an inspirational speaker and published author. I was fortunate to attend a Women Inspiring Women Event here in New Hampshire where Elizabeth was speaking.

While I don't remember Elizabeth's exact words of inspiration, the essence of what I personally got from her exists in my notes.

My inner connection to her story and message brings forth these mindset strengths:

- We all suffer from fears, anxieties, and struggles; it doesn't matter what we've been through;
- What's important is to pull good from those situations so they don't hold you back;
- Build strength in your confidence, courage, and voice in the world to avoid a victim mindset.

This formerly beaten-down young girl was now standing firmly as an articulate, successful adult. Her courage, I believe, lies in her commitment to retell a horrific experience in order to pass on positive lessons to others. Her persevering attitude is infectious.

Courage to Face Personal History

Most of the time, you'll hear the advice that we should stick only to the present. After all, it's all we have. Forget the past, they say. It's gone anyway. The future isn't here yet, so just do your best to get through the day. Is this the best or only way to live a good life? I believe many of us are too stuck in the present, frankly. We fear looking backwards because we might be to blame for how we got where we are in the present. We stay firm in today, exhausted and wondering why our feet are dragging and have paralyzing or ambiguous visions for our future.

One way you can strengthen yourself today is to honor your personal history. No matter how painful it may have been, it doesn't define you. It can serve to teach you important things about yourself. Are you carrying fears that are linked to your past? If so, you can explore your fears in the exercises I provide in this book. This might help alleviate some heavy stress. Just because you've suffered some past hurts doesn't mean you are destined to be a wounded soul in search of healing. It isn't necessary for most of us to endure years of childhood analysis in a therapist's office to ignite a better life or vision of ourselves.

We can experience profound changes by sharing our story for the sake of healing, growth, and helping others. Isn't that what we should all be doing in one way or another? You don't have to have a career in speaking or writing. If it's too painful to talk about your past, seek to understand how your story might benefit others. Then, commit to igniting wisdom from those times. Finally, commit to sharing your stories and lessons with your children. Keep your personal history alive for the sake of connection and wisdom.

Gift of Perseverance #4: Curiosity

"Success comes from curiosity, concentration, perseverance, and self-criticism."

~Albert Einstein

Ghost Father: A Story of Uncertainty

The metal trailer in which we were living seemed to echo the anxious worries that filled my mind. I was imagining my brother's arrival home. I remembered burning my pinky finger on my mother's glass coffee pot once. I must have been about three years old at the time. Now, it was impossible to imagine the kind of pain my brother must be in.

Like little pebbles ricocheting off the walls of my brain, my worries were a nuisance. I attempted to silence my thoughts with pillows held tightly to my ears. Instead, I poked my cheek with a feather that found its way through the pillow case.

I reached out for the on switch to the blue and white table lamp. My sister Pam had left, and I couldn't remember why. All I could see was the vision of our father waving her goodbye in a shoo-away motion while his eyes stayed glued to the newspaper.

Silence was so thick that all I could hear was the racing of my heartbeat. I missed my mother. I rubbed my fingers along her face in a photo of her in an effort to feel her smiling cheeks. Normally, I found peace in the quiet woods of Lyman, but on this night, I felt scared.

Restless, I threw the feather pillow against the wall and kicked off the sheets. I pushed both feet into the slippers at the foot of my bed. As I was making my way down the hall to visit my father, I bit my lip. I was too late. The click of the front door closing told me I was now alone with my little sister, Carol. This was not a new experience, and yet it never failed to make me anxious.

I stood on my tiptoes to catch a view of the glow in the dark clock situated on a wall shelf. It read 10:00p.m. The thought of my little sister alone at the end of the hallway made me leap over a pile of dirty laundry at the side of my bed.

My fingers slid along the walls on either side of me, acting as eyes in the dark. At last, I reached Carol's room. I snuggled beside her and stroked her hair gently. The uncertainty of my father's presence made me think of him as a ghost. He was busy appearing, disappearing, and reappearing. I felt haunted by his regular reminders that I had disappointed him in some way.

I was relieved for the one street light situated at the end of the driveway. I wasn't afraid of the dark, but I knew if I had to reach the neighbor, I had a beacon of light. I wasn't sure if my sister Pam would be coming back. Sometimes she stayed overnight at a friend's house.

My head rested on Carol's pillow. I fell asleep to one question: Is daddy ever coming back?

Behind My Father's Eyes: Empowering Reflections

I have my biological father to thank for my interest in human behavior and psychology. Upon reflection, I realize I also have to thank my father for how I came to learn empathy. I might not have received these gifts had it not been for my father's behavioral choices.

Choosing to become more reflective and curious about your experiences is one of the most empowering things you can do for yourself. This is especially true if someone has hurt or betrayed you. To settle into long-term grief because of someone else's stress response and behavioral choices is to punish yourself further.

This above story illustrates my earliest exposure to emotional distress where my father was concerned. His pattern to abandon was ongoing. I hold no ill will toward his memory and have no resentments. It is my opinion that my father may have suffered a turbulent relationship with all four of our fiery devils. I make no attempt to analyze or confirm why he made some unhealthy choices. As with all the people to whom I refer in this book, I explore my personal behaviors and psychology in response to their influence. This is a healthy form of self-criticism that leads to success in overcoming any lingering emotional turbulence.

If you are afraid of old ghosts, it's difficult to persevere. I hope you will be inspired to reflect and learn from you past. The ghosts of the past may always exist. Your choice is to no longer allow them to haunt you.

CHAPTER 5
HEALING GIFTS AND INNER STRENGTHS

"It turns out that the most delicately perceived things are capable of surviving fires. The people we perceive as strong can get burned badly. We may never know why these things happen. The key is to agree to connect to a strong feeling of faith even as our prayers and questions go unanswered. This is where a higher inner strength and courage are born. This is how fear dissipates."

~Amy McCann

How to Recognize Blessings

- In times when you feel you are at your most delicate point of burning down, you have been blessed to survive.
- You are blessed to have the choice to live forward as a source of hope, love, and light to others.
- A feeling of strength doesn't necessarily appear as a result of praying alone. Blessings are sometimes found in the unanswered prayers.

- Good fortune can be found when you keep faith even in times where things don't make sense.
- In exercising this power within you called faith, you raise hope! Hope is a blessing you can pass on to others.

Today, our family's history lives on in the pages of my mother's photo albums. I visit these periodically. That pungent, unforgettable fire smell never misses a chance to strike the nostrils as you turn each page. Still, it evokes a connection back to hopeful beginnings in the midst of chaos.

You might ask, "Sure, Amy, but where would I look to find hope in my situation?"

In addition to a connection to God or higher energy that might guide you, it is also helpful to access the human angels in your life who have offered you hope.

Ask yourself:

- Who in my life has put their arm around me in an effort to soothe my pain?
- Did this person succeed in making me feel or see things differently?

If so, allow that person to flood your mind and the feeling of comfort to soothe you. This will inspire you to see hope as a more available energy that you can access anytime.

Hope is one of the first life-lasting gifts I received as a child. As you allow your own gifts to shine, you become grounded in the first step to expression of gratitude for all that exists inside of you.

Beneath the Ashes: A Story of Hope

"Hope can exist in the ashes of uncertainty. Be brave to look where it is dark so that you may better hear hope's message."

~Amy McCann

Blowing the black soot off a heap of photos made me sneeze repeatedly. This annoyed me as I strained to see if I what I had found was real. Was this actually a picture of my little sister and me standing beside a Christmas tree? I tiptoed through the ashes to catch a better look. There we were, in 1978 checkered-style pants, each holding a baby doll from Santa. How was it possible that this photo survived the fire? Soon, photo after photo emerged from beneath a layer of ashes.

I swept my head from side to side, scanning for possible evidence that an angel was nearby. To this day, I believe that angels and that spirits of loved ones are close by.

I believe coming across these photos was a good fortune incident. It matched what my sister Pam had said when she tried to comfort me: "Maybe this was God's way of bringing our family closer." She had passed on a life-lasting gift—the gift of hope. Now, squatting above these burnt leftovers, I had evidence that hope existed!

Only a week before, you would have found me kneeling in this same spot, glued to a coloring book. Now, I knew I wasn't supposed to be standing in this fiery mess; it was dangerous to be rifling through burnt debris. But no one was around, and I was curiously fascinated by this treasure I had found.

Soon, a film reel of a television commercial I had filmed the winter before surfaced to the top of the pile. The edges were melted, and it, too, seemed to have magically survived. Beside it lay a charred Christmas card that was produced by the company with which I had filmed the commercial. On the front of this card, you can see me standing in a horse-drawn sleigh smiling widely.

I came across one more photo in the pile of ashes. It was the five McCann siblings posing in front of a pyramid-shaped mountain in the background. As a tear streamed down my cheek, I realized it was because I felt happy. Happy? Perhaps it's because I knew that we had a very cool family, even though we were presently walking through the fires of hell. Perhaps I was too young to recognize this feeling as gratitude to be alive. I believed we were a family of strength.

After a short struggle to pull my foot from between two boards, I decided it was time to leave the ashy rubble. My happy moment ceased a few moments later. I had a vision of our cat, dog, and guinea pigs all running from the devils of fire to hide in the woods.

Another tear dropped. I was back in the dreadful feeling of uncertainty. Could they still be alive? It was possible, and then again, it was also not. This internal turmoil would have lasted longer had I not believed in animal heaven. Instead of running into the woods in hopes of finding my pets, I stumbled through the burnt debris. I wiped my tears on the sleeves of my sweater, which were blackened from the soot.

I made it back to my room and fluffed my pillow in preparation of a nap. Later, I would awaken with excitement to tell my sister all that I had uncovered beneath the ash.

Inner Lesson of Hope

Miracles can arise from the ashes of uncertainty.

Connect to Healing Gifts

This small section might serve to inspire you to use music as a healing tool and to learn, study, and practice visual methods of meditation and relaxation before crisis hits. A daily visual guided meditation generates good feelings and the confidence to handle life as it is thrown at you. It clears the mind and soothes the soul. As you will see, it is also a highly effective tool that can later ease someone's pain if it ever became necessary.

Music Heals the Heart and Soul

One day, with a kitten in my lap, I sat cross-legged in a well-worn brown-colored armchair. This chair had been generously donated by a neighbor. My magical sister Pam bounced cheerfully into the room swinging a guitar she had borrowed from her boyfriend. "I'm recording some songs. Do you and Carol want to sing backup?"

My sister Pam could always be found writing songs, playing the drums, or strumming the guitar. Her singing helped to soothe the sting of our family's predicament. Pam held a strong maternal presence for me. She tended to our skinned knees, told ghost stories, and was a picnic planner extraordinaire. Today, she is a professional singer, songwriter, and musician.

On this day, our mother was away tending to our brother at Shriner's Burn Institute in Boston. We banded together through music to help heal our brother's spirit. This was the beginning of many harmonious and recorded sessions singing the songs of Joni Mitchell, John Denver, James Taylor, and Christopher Cross, to name a few sentimental favorites of the time.

Healing Gift of Appreciation

The act of appreciation is most naturally available, yet somehow, we don't access it enough. Appreciation can serve to ignite the pleasure circuit of your brain. One demonstration could be to honor others while they are living. Don't wait for a grave-site invitation to say all you were too busy to say about a person while he or she was alive. Funerals are not the only places we can or should pay honor to others. Private journals aren't the only way to express gratitude. Let's work to actively generate and live out happier moments.

Our brother Doug listened to these tapes during his recovery. According to our mother, *You've Got a Friend* by James Taylor was one special song my sister sang that seemed to touch our brother. These recordings were played over a loud speaker by a nurse. As the story goes, these songs brought tears to the children and staff in the hospital ward of Shriner's Burn Institute.

Meditation Soothes Burning Pain

In my early teens, my mom described what she called her guided visual journeys. She held these sessions with my brother to help ease his physical pain. This was my first exposure to the power of guided meditation. She explained how she would guide my brother to imagine walking into a cool stream of water. She would then ask him to describe the details of his surroundings. This helped him step outside of his excruciating pain in between his scheduled doses of morphine.

In times of great distress, it is very difficult to think straight. I am certain these sessions served to help my mother think more clearly under such drastic circumstances. As a mother of twin girls, I often held guided meditations with them before they fall off to sleep when they were very little. Now, they listen to their own preference of meditation to help them relax.

Story Connections to Strength

"Our ability to handle life's challenges is a measure of our strength of character."

~Les Brown

Honoring Mother's Strengths

Standing at a height of just 4'11, our mother is a mighty force. A woman whose stress might have toppled others, her survival skills weren't fully appreciated until I hit the age of twelve.

The softness of my mother's hands was the result of handling leather in a factory day in and day out. After working a full day, I recall her returning back to work after she put us to bed. She had a workhorse ethic and a cheery morning disposition. I could never match my mother's cheerfulness upon rolling out of bed.

My mother was fiercely effective in shooting warning expressions of her disappointment in any one of our behaviors. This was the kind of disappointment that sparked and instilled the importance of truth telling and a healthy fear of even trying to voice a white lie. Today, friends still bring up the fact that they knew not to mess with my mom. Still, she was (and is) cherished among close friends as a happy, fun-loving, mighty second mom.

I am grateful to connect to my mother as a friend in my adult years. She and I have spoken often of her struggles throughout the years. There are many life-lasting gifts my mother passed on. Here, I wish to honor her ability to influence me to see myself as a leader. She helped me create paths to personal success by helping me avoid some mistakes.

Gifts of Wisdom from My Mother

It's a burden to think you can try and save the world. Know that you have the power to help many people and work with one person or group at a time to make a real difference. Just don't let it get in the way of what you must do for yourself.

Stay awake to the warning signs of toxic people. If you happen to miss the signs that seem so obvious to others, consider it a flaw you can work with to improve instead of a personal failure that is permanent.

Tell the truth. It is much easier than having to keep track of lies.

Doubt about Honoring Loved Ones

I've spoken with clients who doubt there is value in honoring loved ones. Some people don't see the need or find it difficult to honor parents whom they feel didn't give them the attention they deserved growing up. If you are that person, it is your choice not to honor your parent(s), or anyone else for that matter. I'm not here to tell you it's mandatory. It is your choice to export your type of reactions and responses to these people to see if this is a behavior or thought process that is causing added stress.

Where our behavior is concerned, we want to view ourselves in relation to others with a beginner's mindset. This allows us to begin from a neutral position. It helps to make us less angry, spiteful, or judgmental of ourselves and others for situations gone wrong.

When you are heavily disappointed by the parent hand you were dealt, at the very least, you may wish to explore whether or not you will later regret not talking to or acknowledging that person.

You could also explore whether or not it is time to mentally release a person for past hurts.

If you do choose to mentally let go of someone, you can still choose to find the gift that came out of any hurt they caused you. Whatever way you wish to go on the topic of honoring others to some degree is up to you. The important thing is to do your best not to dishonor others for spite. This does nothing in the way of elevating your peace journey. At the very least, it comes across as unattractive to others.

Blessing in a Small Town: A Story of Good Fortune

One of the strange miracles in all of this mess was that this factory where my mom worked was directly across the street from our home.

This might not appear to be a big deal or a blessing, except that we lived in the middle of nowhere. Our journey to this tiny New Hampshire town of Lyman from the Boston area happened after my father took a job as a radio host in Littleton, New Hampshire. Following the fire, he was unemployed, and our family no longer had a car. Thankfully, my mother had a job at the factory and took a full-time position to keep our family well fed and taken care of.

It would have been a lager headache to try to find a way to work out of town. These were the days when cell phones and the internet didn't exist. Before job search engines, it was less easy to search for employment. This factory was owned by the same neighbors whose kitchen window gave me my first vision of my brother.

In winter, it was almost impossible to drive the curvy, steep roads of Lyman. There were so few people, it was rare to see a car pass by. Since traffic was non-existent, we took advantage of the open country roads. Imagine a toboggan weighed down by five kids and hitched to the back of a station wagon. This was my father's idea of an adventure—pulling us up the snowy hill. It was not the safest adventure, but we had a blast, and we all survived.

In summer, we could be seen marching down our country road, fully donned in parade costumes, instruments, and batons. Some days, we drew chalk squares on the pavement to play hopscotch.

Nature was my playground, and I would often skip off to be alone in the woods. I had a favorite rock that became my secret station where I would write about all my hopes, dreams, and worries in my journal.

Our farmhouse that would eventually burn down came with a mountain view and plenty to do in nature. I was born and lived in Colorado for the first two years of life until our move to Massachusetts. Lyman, however, is my hometown where I grew up. I imagined us to be like the Walton family. *The Waltons* was a television show about a close-knit family living in the country in the Depression era. I could connect with some of the struggles and fun times the characters had.

Before our family's house fire, I saw a rerun episode where the Walton's house caught fire. It scared me so much that I feared our house might burn down, too. When that came to life, a new worry bloomed. What if every fear comes true?

While our family worked to rebuild, we camped out in a loaner camper yards away from where our home once stood.

The owners of this leather goods factory located directly across the street hired my mother as their first employee. She assisted in helping the business get up and running. We felt like rich people when she gifted us leather purses that didn't make the design cut for fancy shops in NYC.

Back on that day at Shriner's Hospitals for Children, our mother placed her soft hands on her two youngest daughters. Things were moving too quickly at this point for her to ease our worries fully. It would be just moments before our brother would appear in a wheelchair.

Strength in Spite of Tragic Events: A Reflection of Strong Character

"A simple act of honoring yourself or someone you admire can immediately take the fire off our stress."

~Amy McCann

My brother Doug was my first role model in compassion, tolerance, truthfulness, and integrity. He is neither a victim of a past injury nor is he strong because of his wounds. He is someone who is emotionally strong in spite of being injured at the age of fifteen.

This book began with a picture of his struggle from my perspective. Today I look to my brother as the voice of reason in many situations. In your life, is there someone with whom you can let your guard down and ask for some reasonable visions into your situation? If so, remember this person the next time you feel stuck.

Quick Card Check-In: Inner Strengths

Based on the types of strengths my brother demonstrates for me, here are some questions you may wish to reflect upon and measure.

Awareness of Behavior: On a 1-10 scale, how **compassionate** have I been lately?

Mindfulness of Reactions: On a 1-10 scale, how **tolerant** do I feel I am with others?

Connection to Inner Self: On a 1-10 scale, how **truthful** have I been about my feelings concerning uncertainty?

Awareness of Integrity: On a scale of 1-10, how confident do I feel when it comes to my level of integrity — am I a trustworthy confidant? Can others trust me to influence them positively as a leader, coach, teacher?

Proactive Life Mastery Academy™
Amy McCann Coaching™

Prepare to Ignite Strength

As you've seen in the previous stories, I gained specific gifts that helped me adjust more positively through uncertain times. Now, it's your turn to connect with some of the gifts of wisdom and lessons you learned from others along the way. This is a foundational and grounding step in moving you toward success. Let's work to ignite and build some strengths in perseverance.

CHAPTER 6
LIGHT UP STRONG HABITS

I've already shown you ways I was able to ignite feelings of good fortune through adversity in the stories I've shared. As a reminder, I felt more fortunate because I learned to:

- Connect to others' struggles in the moment to feel less alone;
- Shift perspective to diminish fear;
- View compassion as something that can ease everyone's pain;
- Appreciate the healing results of music and meditation.

Soon you'll learn to ignite strong habits and put them into action in your own life.

First, let's take a look at your Pyramid of Perseverance Diagram™ to see where it is we are headed!

First Level Perseverance – Gratitude & Grace

Welcome to your Pyramid of Perseverance diagram. This is where we are headed!

Pyramid of Perseverance:
Amy McCann Coaching (AMC) Proactive Levels to Success™

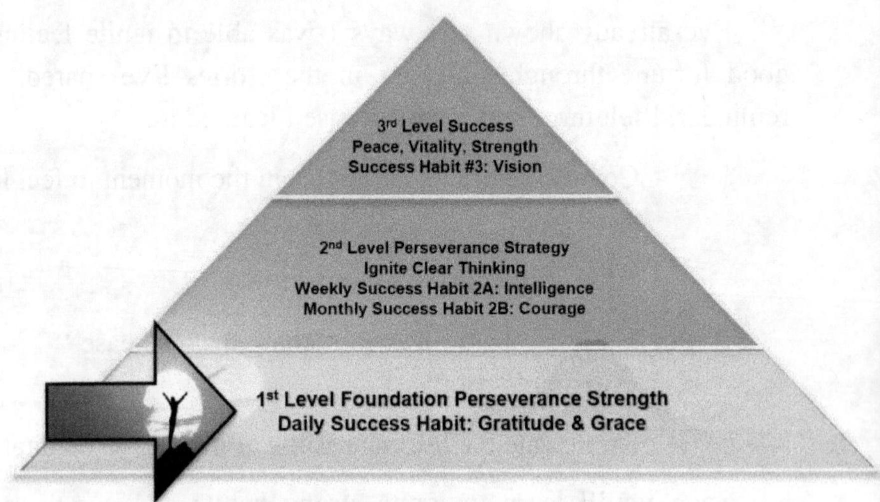

Proactive Life Mastery Academy™ Amy McCann Coaching™
Proactive Life Mastery Academy™ Online Training in Perseverance

Habit #1: Visual Trigger to Light Up Daily Gratitude

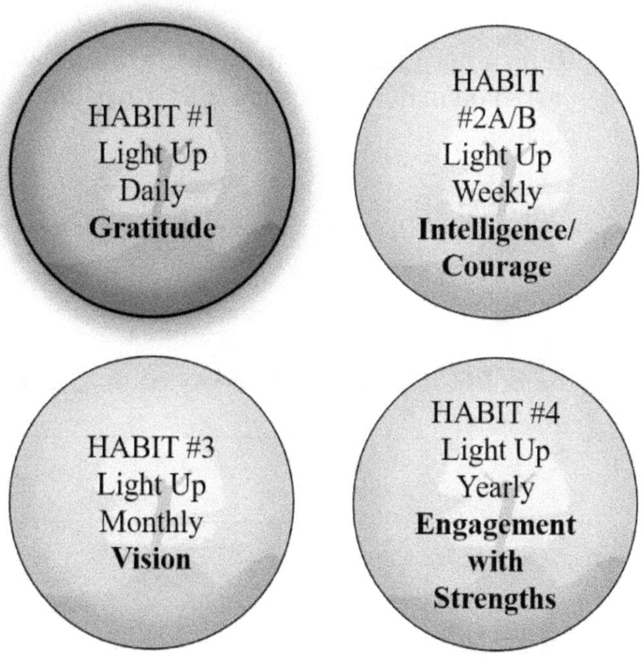

*Adapted from Proactive Life Mastery Academy™ Online Training in Perseverance

Imagine this as your stovetop. You likely cook every day, but even if you hate cooking, you may never look at a stovetop the same. Imagine lighting each burner with these success habits.

If visual diagrams don't work for you, just post the word GIVE on your refrigerator to remind you to light up gratitude, intelligence, vision, and engagement with your strengths.

These habits are meant to help you persevere and are proactive in your effort to move better through uncertain times.

HABIT #1: LIGHT UP DAILY GRATITUDE AND GRACE WORKSHEET

1) **Remember and Record:** One time in life when someone passed on major life-lasting gifts of wisdom, knowledge, or change.

   Time and Place:______________________________

   Name of Person:______________________________

   Major life-lasting gift passed to me that helped me face adversity: ______________________________

   ____

   ____

   ____

2) **Recall and Write Down:** What is one emotion I felt when this person passed on this lesson?

   ____

   ____

   ____

   ____

3) Narrow Down: What can I connect this gift to today to ignite graceful appreciation of this person?

____

____

____

____

Adapted from Proactive Life Mastery Academy™ Online Training in Perseverance

Congratulations!

You've begun the process of building a foundation of strong habits. This helps you stay connected in gratitude for all that exists inside of you. Now, you can use the card below to add an action step.

Gratitude Action Step*

A simple action plan to ignite a habit of living gratitude.

Purpose

Daily acts of appreciation light up a more graceful presence in you. A personal foundation in perseverance and success begin with living in grace to others.

This Quick Card Check-In with Gratitude and Grace is also included in the Proactive Planning Guide.

Quick Card Check-In: Gratitude and Grace

Example: I will *call Gina* to say thanks for the confidence exercise she taught me and how it helped me earn my promotion at work.

Grace Example: I will speak the word grace in my mind each time I feel myself getting anxious around my bossy co-worker.

Day 1:______________________________

Day 2:______________________________

Day 3:______________________________

Day 4:______________________________

Day 5:______________________________

Proactive Life Mastery Academy™
Amy McCann Coaching™

Adapted from Amy McCann Coaching™ Proactive Life Mastery Academy™ Online Training in Perseverance

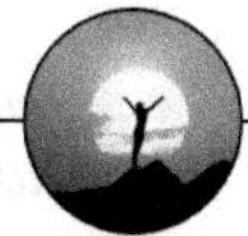

Stop Pushing Forward...Start Flowing Forward

Now that you've experienced a taste of how to ignite gratitude through uncertainty, let's keep this journey flowing. Let's agree to stop pushing so hard and move away from unhealthy struggles.

Moving forward, we will explore the following:

- Your Stress response
- The benefits of living a proactive lifestyle
- Uncertainty and disappointment
- A whole health check-in
- Some burning habits to extinguish

Types of Stress Response

It's not stress that kills us, it is our reaction to it.

~Hans Selye

It so happens that the scenes I shared in Chapter 1 conveniently illustrate a picture of the three most common types of stress responses referred to by psychologists as fight, flight, and freeze.

Since this book isn't about pumping you with information, I won't bore you with easily accessible information about these three types of stress. Let's simply tie them to the fiery story in Chapter 1.

Freeze Response
My grandmother fainting; my feeling like the tin man, unable to move.

Flight Response
My "magical" sister's flight on a stairway with a broken leg and four little girls in her arms.

Fight Response
My uncle saving my brother's life despite his risk of getting injured.

YOUR PERSONAL STRESS RESPONSE ASSESSMENT

How Do I Respond When I'm Faced with Uncertainty?

A. I generally feel like I'm in quicksand when I think about my next step in life.

B. I typically run away from situations that might add overwhelming uncertainty to my plate.

C. I generally fight against uncertainty and look for ways to feel more certain about how things will unfold.

Now, repeat this exercise to connect to your stress response to fear, doubt, and disappointment.

Now that you're more in touch with your stress response in relation to the Fiery Four, you'll know better moving ahead whether you might fall into a frozen state of fear, will be more likely to run for the hills, or might fight to the death to stay standing.

Awareness about yourself is key to any growth. It isn't helpful to think heavily about this. Just stick with your most typical stress response as of late and adjust as necessary as life changes.

A Way Out of Stress Asks

Is it best for me to keep running away from relationships because I've been disappointed more than twice?

Am I tired of feeling stuck when it comes to figuring out what I want to do at this stage of life?

Proactive Life Mastery Academy™ Amy McCann Coaching™

Ignite Today for a Brighter Tomorrow: Proactive vs. Reactive Lifestyle

Process over Perfection

Be proactive. This is your new mantra. To be proactive is the number-one habit of highly effective people, according to the late Stephen Covey. His book, *The Seven Habits of Highly Effective People*, helped me align to what I was already practicing proactively and what I needed to improve on through a difficult stage of life.

So, what does it mean to be highly effective in your own life? Here, it means being responsible in your commitment to better handle the devils of uncertainty, doubt, fear, and disappointment. It means embracing process over perfection. It is about building purpose, process, and progress throughout your life.

Remember, to be proactive is to prepare for things before they happen. This doesn't mean we are building a crystal ball into the future. However, we are most definitely in control of how we respond today so that we can better predict how we will handle tomorrow's surprises.

The idea here is this: In building a stronger version of ourselves (which includes necessary mindset and behavioral changes), we will be able to lift the heavy piles of dirt more easily as life chooses to dump them on us. Uncertain times are inevitable, so let's do well to avoid dumping unnecessary uncertainty on ourselves in the meantime.

Since we can't see into the future, we can choose to do two things:

- Accept the ambiguity of life;
- Laugh in the face of disappointment as often as possible.

Clear Your Mind

Everything with which you engage in this book is moving you closer to generating a clearer mind in order to ignite peace and personal success. As a Certified High Performance Coach, the number-one high performance habit I learned through the High Performance Institute is to seek clarity. According to Brendon Burchard, New York Times Best Selling Author of *High Performance Habits: How Extraordinary People Become That Way,* "High performers are more successful than their peers, yet they are less stressed."

Let's work to move you closer to being a less stressed, more successful person in all areas of life.

Start Small, Strong Habits

"No matter how small you start, start something that matters."

~ Brendon Burchard

Imagine the day you no longer feel emotionally paralyzed by uncertainty. Here are some common reasons people experience paralyzing uncertainty:

- Divorce
- Job Loss
- New Business Venture
- Stage of Life Change
- Disability

If you are facing any of these challenges, you might be confused about what to do first. All of these challenges create high levels of uncertainty and doubt. At the same time, you might feel disappointed that you aren't able to make any clear decisions due to all the stress you feel. The key is to start small. You matter, so it makes sense to begin by connecting to yourself first.

To get you moving and thinking more clearly, you can choose to lower the flame of uncertainty within you. To do this, you must be courageously dedicated to checking into your spiritual, emotional, physical, and environmental health. Without attention to these things, you will remain stuck. When you check in daily, you gain clarity of your personal development. Clarity helps you make better decisions. Some struggle (discomfort) is necessary for growth, we just want to remove unnecessary struggles that wear you down.

So, how do you accomplish this when so much responsibility lies in front of you? Follow the simple one-page Whole Health Check-In. Life doesn't have to be so hard if you start small, strong habits.

WHOLE HEALTH JOURNAL WORKSHEET

INITIATE: Spiritual Health

How will I activate my gratitude today? ____________

____

____

In what area of life do I lack faith today? Which one of the Fiery Four Devils might be behind my lack of faith? ______

____

____

What inner gift of wisdom can I access to help me initiate faith? ________________________________

____

CALIBRATE: Emotional/Physical

What negative and positive emotions do I feel today? What is one healthy choice I can make to change/keep these emotions?

____

____

____

What physical pain or ease do I feel today? What is one healthy choice I can make to change/keep these?______________

____

____

CONTEMPLATE: Mental/Environmental

How does my physical environment make me feel today? __

___

___

What is one move I could make in my environment to ignite a greater feeling of energy and calm? ___

___

___

CELEBRATE: Whole Health Progress

How do I choose to celebrate my whole health progress of checking in? ___

___

___

Adapted from Amy McCann Coaching™ Proactive Life Mastery Academy™
Online Training in Perseverance
Proactive Life Mastery Academy™ Amy McCann Coaching™

Fiery Disappointment Burns

"Disappointment can work to harden you.
Persevering strength works to toughen you."

~Amy McCann

On the first day of the commercial shoot, I took my place in the sleigh. It was the winter prior to the house fire. Tightly bundled in my blue snow suit, I was instructed to listen to the voice coming from the oversized earpiece the producer had wiggled in. I was told the voice would to tell me where to turn my head and when to smile and cue me to speak my lines.

My father had taken me to an audition for this national commercial a week before. To his expectance, I landed the role. Immediately, my chest tightened as my father professed to the producers to be my acting manager. He referred to this experience as my "big break." I felt a mix of excitement and distress. At the same time, it was an opportunity that might allow my father to stick around and visit with me. As it turned out, this was my first big meeting with the devil to which we are referring as disappointment.

The filming covered a period of three days. I was most excited to miss three days of school. Plus, I got to ride in a sleigh pulled by the famous Clydesdale horses. Many hours later, my hands were frozen to the back of the sleigh driver's seat. The most warming highlight of the day was my chance to visit with and pet the horses. A cheery makeup artist gossiped about her adventures in the television industry and her difficulties in dealing with "rude actors." Overall, the first day of filming proved to be fun. I smiled on cue, spoke my lines, and managed not to freeze to death in the icy temperatures of northern New Hampshire.

Halfway through the second day, I managed to ignite my father's anger. His disappointment in me burned brightly in his cheeks—enough to melt the snow. I could swear he had grown horns as he bent down to yell in my face. My joy was about to be interrupted.

"What were you thinking? You've ruined everything!" he barked. What brought about this fiery devil of disappointment in my father? A one-minute nap. Somehow, I managed to fall asleep while filming. I was so far gone, I was deaf to the voices in my earpiece. A journey into dreamland infuriated my father so much that he told me this was the end of any chance to go further with my "career" as an actress.

A man from the light crew put his arm around me and led me to the makeup trailer. There, I was instructed to rest. Another crew member assured me he would come back when it was time to film again. A loud bang on the door made me clutch a nearby pillow. My father appeared with one hand on his hip and a cigarette in the other. He walked three steps to stand above me. He sneered, "What do you think you're doing, taking a rest? You have to get back out there before they fire you!"

The gossipy makeup lady appeared behind my father the moment he was giving me a lesson in how much I had disappointed him. Pointing her finger to the door, she silently and swiftly instructed my father to leave at once. He obeyed, and the trailer door slammed shut. Tears streamed down my face. I asked if it was true what my father said. Were they going to fire me? She gently hugged me. This is how I remember her response:

"Nonsense! I'm surprised it took you two days to fall asleep! It's a lot of work for a girl your age, especially in all this icy cold weather! No, you're not fired. But you will be replaced by the producer's son for that brief turn around scene, so we can finish out the day. No one will know it's not you because he's about your size, and we will be filming his backside. I do need you to dry your tears because we will need your bright, shiny smile in all the other scenes when we shoot tomorrow. Can you do that for me?" As I nodded, she added, “Oh, and we’ll need to borrow your snow suit for the fill-in to wear. I have some extra clothes you can borrow in the meantime.”

I didn’t see my father again except at a dinner that was held for cast and crew members. As I slurped on warm tomato soup, I was grateful that my father chose to punish me with a silent treatment. He puffed on his cigarette in a corner far away from the dining table with his legs crossed, staring blankly at a wall.

A Takeaway Reflection

The story I just shared highlights what we’ve all been through: being disappointed by others or disappointing them. Unfortunately, my father’s behavior during that three-day shoot was not an isolated incident. Still, it isn’t my place or intention to throw him under the bus.

Anytime I reflect on a memory that involves my father, I become more open to imagining the possibility of his deep inner struggles. It reminds me that while it was once tempting to call him the devil himself, he was, in fact, a human being. His efforts to connect with me were sporadic and stressful at best. However, in honor of lighter moments, he made an ordinary kindergarten apple picking trip a memory to treasure.

I suspect he was hurting himself far longer than he ever hurt me. This is, of course, only my opinion. I neither feel sorry for him nor defend him. I’ve simply come to observe his behavior with curiosity and possibility. Although there may have been more negative than positive moments from my perspective, I get to choose which moments teach me something and which ones I choose to simply cherish close to my heart. This brings a kind of personally elevated peace to my soul. You can choose to do the same if a more peaceful heart is your mission.

In my mind, I've had a secret bond with my father, as we share what I believe to be a biological struggle with depression. I have been to dark places that once brought me private shame and fear. I can only imagine my father went to these places more often than not. Simply contemplating this has helped me develop a stronger self-love and distant compassion for my father, who passed away a couple of years ago.

I've learned to respect my bouts of depression and have come to fully believe that they no longer own me. It is a part of me, from which I can learn. To connect to depression publicly is a spiritual kind of strength. As I breathe in all that I am, I become a more relaxed, confident, and peaceful person. I am no longer afraid of who I am. I believe my beliefs about my father have a lot to do with that.

You might ask, "Why should I waste time considering someone else's struggle? The answer is you don't have to at all. You are a free-thinking person. It is only one suggestion to help clear your mind to possible ways of thinking about your life experience.

If you can keep in mind that everyone is suffering at some level, heartache associated with disappointment can begin to slip away. Wouldn't it be a relief to finally release these emotional attachments to make way for better understanding and brighter days ahead? Who in your life might you choose to become more curious about?

This story leads me to our next section, where we will explore how to ignite grace in the face of resentment.

Grace Extinguishes Resentment

"There are no justified resentments."

~Dr. Wayne Dyer

One antonym of grace is neglect. If we are stuck in feelings of resentment, we serve to neglect ourselves. When we are neglectful, it becomes impossible to be graceful. Grace is the foundation and ignition of our journey. It is what helps us breathe deeper and persevere well.

Burning Down Conclusions

How often do you conclude something negative about someone because of the way they've behaved? You might say this person deserves it if their bad behavior has been repeated numerous times. You might feel justified in blaming a person for years to come because they served to burn down your hopes and dreams. If you've chosen to put this person in a mental grave, you might still carry a heavy pain if you've been abandoned.

If you've ever been abandoned by someone, you most likely searched for others who could understand or feel sympathy for your pain. After all, most of your friends will jump on board to agree that this person was less than kind or loving toward you.

It's a very lonely feeling to know that someone has chosen to leave you, isn't it? This is especially painful if it is a parent. Although it is painful, the act of a parent (or anyone) leaving you can become a most unique opportunity to begin loving yourself. This isn't an easy thing to do if you're convinced you aren't lovable. Then again, we're not here to walk on easy street.

The first thing is to check in with the types of conclusions you draw about yourself. This takes the focus off of the other person and onto you again. If you conclude you're not meant to be happy, you are out of vibration with grace. Ask yourself the following questions.

- Who do I believe I am?
- What kind of future do I see for myself when it comes to relationships?

When someone abandons us, the feeling of resentment can burn inside us for years. The taste of bitterness can sting our tongues and work to evoke angry words. Worse, we can begin to resent ourselves for not having any direction forward. How could we have been so stupid to be hurt so badly by an ex? As a woman, you might resent your father for your inability to trust men. You probably want out of this type of misery, but the devil of fear might be why you aren't able to move forward. What if you get burned again? You might say, "I can't marry my girlfriend. What if she leaves me like my mother did?"

Fear can lead to fixed and negative beliefs about yourself. If fear has been your devil drawing burning conclusions, why not try turning those conclusions into something positive? Are you ready to build a foundation of grace?

Proactive Method to Extinguish Conclusions

One client with whom I met wanted to work through her resentments. She had a goal to become clear-minded and loving toward herself. She was looking to ignite new purpose in her life. We were to meet for five sessions in a Package Your Purpose™ course I designed a few years back.

With the end in mind, I first opened our session with an outline to achieve two things in the coach/client relationship:

MY COACH GOALS:

1) Gain clarity into her present feelings.

2) Help ignite a new vision of her future desired self.

MY CLIENT GOALS:

1) Draw out awareness of present paralyzing beliefs based in emotion.
2) Move away from resentment and into a new purpose that begins with self-care.

This Proactive Method Outline was broken down in ABC fashion:

Active Beliefs

Bitterness Description

Conclusion Statement

Here is how this client's journey played out and how you can turn your conclusions around:

PRESENT VISION OF MYSELF (in relation to resentment):

Active Negative Belief About Self: I believe I can't be happy because my ex took my trust away.

Bitterness Description (one emotion to describe): I feel angry.

Conclusion Statement (combine A+B to create a sentence): I believe I can't be happy because my ex took my trust away, and this makes me feel angry.

FUTURE DESIRED VISON OF MYSELF:

Active Belief About Myself: I believe in my ability to be happy.

Bitterness Description (In a sentence, use one positive emotion that extinguishes bitterness): I no longer feel angry toward my ex because I've learned to be kind toward myself.

Conclusion Statement (combine A+B to create your desired future vision of yourself):

I believe in my ability to be happy because I have learned to be kinder toward myself and no longer feel angry.

Once we gained vision into present pain and future desire to ignite new emotion, this client was no longer paralyzed by the behaviors of her ex. This client proved to herself that she is a success in perseverance.[1]

Wisdom to Share

One of my favorite spiritual mentors is the late Dr. Wayne Dyer. One night, he was giving a seminar on his Ten Principles to Manifestation. The third principle stood out, and was to me, the most profound. It was titled: There Are No Justified Resentments. He explained that he had borrowed this phrase, and I'd like to borrow it here for our purposes. It may prove to be a challenging phrase honor, but it can spark movement out of bitterness. Judgments about others and harboring resentments take a lot of mental energy. When it comes to being stronger mental energy is something we should generate, not deplete. Don't you deserve to feel vibrant again?

[1] In case you feel it's impossible to let go of the pain of abandonment or betrayal, you may request a link to receive a partial summary of a successful student journey report to amy@amymccann.life Type the following in the subject line: "Student Journey Request:Persevere to Succeed."

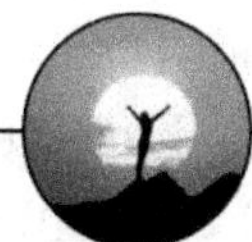

Student Journey Request Info

To set the stage for you, this was a five-week group coaching series. This student volunteered to be our "in the moment" case study for a week. This session was designed to help students walk themselves through an impromptu method of stress reduction I designed and guided this group through the process.

Student Testimonial:

"Amy's group coaching session was 'life changing!' I now have the tools I need to help manage what used to make my 'head spin!' Looking forward to the next meeting, as I wouldn't miss it for anything. I left feeling more confident than I have in a long time!"

~ Group Coaching Student

Clarity to Extinguish Jealousy

"Oh, what a bitter thing it is to look into happiness through another man's eyes."

~William Shakespeare

If judgements are a form of resentment, most of us know that jealousy can also serve to burn us from the inside out. This feeling can put you in a sticky jam and feels anything but peaceful.

When you're in a jam of jealousy, of course it helps to reprogram. Jealousy is an insecure emotion that screams discomfort. The good news is that growth requires some discomfort. Using the ABC outline I used with my client, try this in your journal as an exercise out of jealousy.

When jealousy rears its ugly head again, you're more likely to move out of it more quickly because you took time to explore it in writing. When you write things down, you are an active participant in your life, which helps you feel more in control. The ability to feel in control of your emotions helps you more readily face any one of the Fiery Four Devils of which we speak in this book.

With a clearer mind you will persevere.

Sample Journal Statement

PRESENT VISION OF JEALOUSY

Active Belief: Jealousy is hard to overcome.

Bitterness Description: I feel anxious when jealousy comes into my life.

Conclusion: I feel jealousy is hard to overcome, and this makes me feel anxious.

FUTURE VISION OF JEALOUSY

I want to feel and be seen as a person of grace, not jealousy. What is one action I can take that helps me show up as a person of grace more often so that I can feel less jealous in the future?

Sample Statement About Jealousy:

Active Belief: Jealousy does not control me.

Bitterness Description: I feel confident in the face of jealousy because I've learned to control my bitterness.

Conclusion: I feel jealousy that does not control me, and I feel confident in the face of any future jealousy because there is no longer a need for bitterness.

PART I SUMMARY

Congratulations! Part I is complete! You've accomplished the following intelligent actions to ignite peace:

- ✓ Lit up grace through daily gratitude
- ✓ Identified a major life-lasting gift to appreciate
- ✓ Completed the Personal Stress Response Assessment
- ✓ Completed the Whole Health Worksheet
- ✓ Learned to extinguish burning habits in resentment and jealousy
- ✓ Secured a first-level foundational purpose to build life-lasting Pyramid of Perseverance

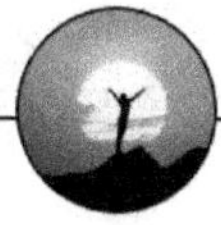

ACTION

Drink in your progress and water your house plants or garden flowers to lift your environment and spirit.

PART II: UNCERTAINTY STRIKES TWICE

LEVEL 3:
Success
Through and Beyond
Uncertainty, Fear, Doubt,
and Disappointment

LEVEL 2:
Strategies
Clear the Mind and Secure Confidence

LEVEL 1:
Strength to Persevere

CHAPTER 7 PARALYZING LESSONS IN STRESS

Persevering New Beginnings

A female nurse wearing red-framed glasses sat slouched behind a blue front desk. I was in a hospital in Kingston, Ontario. She was wearing a faded blue-toned set of scrubs. I scratched my head in irritation at her tapping of a pencil. I bit the remains of a hangnail from my right thumb. My chest tightened as each tip of the pencil lead met the glossy desk top.

Whips of gray hair blew across the nurse's forehead as she switched from tapping to fanning her face with a pizza brochure. In agonizing repetition, she continued to wave the stained faux fan. By this time, my face was warm with impatience. The photo of a 12-inch pizza was making my stomach curdle.

I inhaled sharply. The janitor's mop sloshed from one side of the floor to the other. That sound began to swish inside my head until it saturated my brain. This brought rise to a headache.

My limbs went numb as a heavy-set doctor approached. An invisible vine of dread seemed to wrap around my chest. It briefly squeezed the breath out of me. As quickly as he approached, this doctor rushed past.

My breath escaped fast past my lips, and I felt as if I might faint. I recalled the day my grandmother fainted under stress. In a silly effort to stay balanced, I gripped the bottom of my skirt tightly.

With an empty stomach and low blood pressure to boot, I figured I was in the best place to be if I were to collapse suddenly.

The nurse at last raised her eyes above her red glasses. She tilted her head downward. My body swayed as if drunk. I'm certain my voice cracked as I braved my question. "Can I see him now?"

Back to tapping the pencil, the nurse scanned her chart. She then gave a nod to indicate that the large clock hand was indeed covering the twelve. Was there a cruel nature hiding behind that blue-faded uniform? I thought to myself, "Aren't nurses supposed to be caring?" In my naiveté, I hadn't yet learned that many nurses are often overworked and sleep deprived. With weary breath, I whispered, "Thank you."

During a brief, unsteady walk down the hospital corridor, my eye caught room number 365. "Three hundred sixty-five days in a year," I pondered. I thought, "How could I possibly know if he would make it through to the end of the year?"

As I reached the door frame of the hospital room entrance, the room was brightly lit. Who was responsible for these glaring lights? My instincts pushed me to flipping two light switches off. A dimmer lit room appeared more inviting and dignified. The numbness of my limbs seemed to prepare me for what my eyes would meet—a motionless figure lying twelve feet in front me.

In between the monitors beeping in unison, my eyes squinted. I strained to take in this very still, eerily frozen person. Still breathing, this man was no longer able to raise his hand and wave hello. His eyes were mostly swollen shut, and I felt compelled to wipe his eyes.

This man I loved was my boyfriend of three years. Just like a day so many years back, tears stung my cheeks as they flowed to meet my lips. Only this time, I was a twenty-three-year-old adult. This time, I was not locked in a tin-man state of paralysis. Still, I was heavily dosed up in stress-numbing chemicals created by this shocking scene.

Images flashed through my mind. I remembered our walk through the park just weeks before. The park was located steps from our three-story apartment in New Jersey. It became almost too hard to bear this memory. The stairwell to the home we had shared would never again support the echo of his feet hitting each step as they rose to the third-level apartment.

I extinguished this vision quickly. It seemed my mind was playing cruel tricks. I could clearly envision my boyfriend running alongside me. I could imagine days past as we challenged each other through the park's obstacle course. I was immediately grieving the memory of his physically animated sense of humor, his jumping up and down with a bathroom plunger years ago, sending my roommate Karyn and me into uncontrollable laughter.

These historical and recent memories tortured me. Then, just as on that day in a burn unit at Shriner's Hospital, I began to immediately reframe my vision of loss into a vision of hopeful possibilities.

Afraid I might lose my balance, I managed to lift my body weight up by the rail of the partially raised hospital bed. I noticed a bright green fluid flowing through a chest tube. It looked like the angry Grinch broken down into puke-colored particles.

The song, *The Grinch*, spouted in my brain: "You nauseate me, Mr. Grinch, with a nauseous super naus…"

The numbing adrenaline flowing throughout my body made it easy to miss that I had bitten off another hangnail. My ring finger was now bleeding. A tiny droplet of blood began to trickle down the side of my palm.

Leaning gently over the bedrail, I managed to give a light kiss to his forehead. I gently caressed the cheeks of this man I loved. I whispered aloud what I felt in my heart: "It's a new beginning."

Devastating uncertainty had struck for the second time in my life to someone I deeply loved. Life once again proved to be cruelly unpredictable.

Journey to the Hospital

I had made it to the Big Apple to work in professional theatre after graduating from the American Academy of Dramatic Arts. My boyfriend and I had been living in New Jersey for the past three years. After a daily morning train ride, I walked for miles through Manhattan each day to avoid the smelly subway. I loved this gritty lifestyle and freedom to be artistic. This life suited me well.

Overall, I loved the city's energy. I loved that I proved to the theatre director from the Vermont college I attended that a small-town girl can actually survive the mean streets of Manhattan. Prior to that most devastating scene in the hospital, I had been rehearsing for many hours for a play.

You might recall I had been rehearsing the voice of Kermit the Frog from a cardboard stage before I was swept down a staircase by my magical sister so many years ago. It seemed a real-life drama had once again chosen to knock at my door to interrupt my playtime.

At the time, I was briefly staying in a basement apartment in Brooklyn. I was in the middle of working out a deal with cockroaches in the bathtub when I received the call that would change everything for the next fifteen years.

It wasn't a call to audition for the role of a lifetime on Broadway. Still, it turned into a dramatic hospital visit as the introductory scene to the biggest role I would accept in real life—the role of a full-time caregiver.

After many annoying rings, I picked up the phone. My senses were heightened and dulled at the same time as I heard these words on the other end of the line: “The doctors don’t know if he’ll make it.”

Perseverance Ignites

"I think a hero is an ordinary individual who finds strength to persevere and endure in spite of overwhelming obstacles."

~Christopher Reeve

A Revisit to Struggle Connection

The week prior to my boyfriend Kevin's injury, Christopher Reeve, the actor best known for his role as Superman, suffered a permanent spinal cord injury in a horse-riding accident. *Superman* was the first movie I ever saw at a movie theatre. I went along on my big sister's date with her boyfriend. I was so little to be sitting in such a big theatre seat that my body was immediately folded in half. I recall my sister's boyfriend keeping one hand securely on my seat during the entire movie so that I wouldn't get lost in the crack of the seat.

Superman was a childhood hero. As an adult, the actor was becoming a hero to me in real life. I knew no one else in my life outside of my boyfriend who had a spinal cord injury. I didn't know of one couple dealing with this kind of unfolding devastation. So, it was a sort of bittersweet gratefulness to be able to connect to the Reeve story as it played out in the media.

Mr. Reeve's optimism was undeniably contagious, and his wife Dana, was an equally positive role model. I will forever be sad that they both passed away and that I never took the chance to thank them for offering such hope from a distance.

Soon, as our story unfolded, I could see that my boyfriend was also a heroic example of perseverance. With so many obstacles staring him in the face, he could be found tutoring injured patients who were still attending school. The nursing staff often commented on his strength in attitude.

Learning to Embrace Absurdity

"A choice to ignite moments of joy in the face of overwhelming stress, loss, or challenges takes courage. To recognize and embrace absurdity in things is to intentionally ignite humor through darkness. To choose to be stronger today than you were yesterday in this way, is a kind of life-lasting personal success."

~Amy McCann

When dark notes play repeatedly in your life, it's not so easy to recognize the lighter notes that accompany them. I want to prepare you to gain *confidence* to set some intentional brighter notes to your situation.

Uncertainty can paralyze you to the point of becoming so serious you lose hope. Everyday life can become more challenging than it has to be when you aren't able to find the humor through major transitions.

One way to create harmony across all areas of your life is to agree to embrace the absurdity of things along the way. I promise you, there are plenty of things (and people) you can find amazingly absurd who will alleviate the pain of your situation.

Steel Magnolias, one of my favorite movies, deals with death and grieving process. I love the characters' abilities to see the absurd in a most grim and permanent situation. Laughter alleviates the overwhelming uncertainty, fear, doubt, and disappointment that accompanies such heavy loss. I've learned that tears of sadness and loss can and should be accompanied by healthy humor and healing laughter. I have also learned that tears aren't always possible or a necessary function of the grieving process. It is not our position to judge others for the way in which they grieve. It is a sacred, personal experience.

If you want to connect to a more harmonious relationship with all emotions as they emerge, think of the most beautiful symphony you've heard. It is filled with dark and light notes. These are the works of art that move us to feel the entirety of our emotions. Any beautiful work of art accomplishes this. Since you are here to create your own life, consider yourself an artist in embracing the humor inside of any burning pain you might feel.

How to Ignite Humor in Uncertain Circumstances

Humor is everything when it comes to facing the most overwhelming circumstances. If you want to face uncertainty with confidence, you must be willing to recognize the absurdity that comes along with major changes

Absurd Dining Experience: A Story to Inspire Humor

"Disappointment is an endless wellspring of comedy inspiration."

~Martin Freeman

There was still so much ahead of us to endure as a couple, and Kevin's sense of humor helped us deal with the many potentially embarrassing and undignified situations that arose.

Almost a year following his injury, we were at a restaurant celebrating his twenty-sixth birthday. In what could have turned out to be an embarrassing scene, my boyfriend made a light, humorous situation. It was a bonus that everyone laughed, but this wasn't his reason for adding light to the situation. He really did have a gift for embracing the absurd, which is a *choice in strength* I hope you'll consider.

With partial arm movement and no hand function, it was a battle to balance rice on a fork, let alone succeed at tasting it. The fork was Velcro-fastened to a medical utensil holder positioned on his forearm. Back then, getting food to the mouth was a major accomplishment. Still, he had a way to go in mastering this task. As if to mock his efforts, the grains of rice took a leap off the fork and onto the center of his lap and thighs. In a struggle to scoop the rice back onto the fork, his body had another plan.

In an injury-related body spasm, my boyfriend's arms flailed wildly and uncontrollably. His right leg kicked out in front as if it were ready to meet the face of a soccer ball. The prongs from the fork successfully caught the grains of rice that were now dancing in the air. The rice was flung straight across the room and directly into the plate of an elderly woman and the hair of her companion. It was the first time we would come to embrace the potential absurdity that could arise in adjusting to normal daily activities of living.

Although I can't recall the exact way Kevin handled this, he showed no embarrassment or frustration. I do remember that he apologized and made some kind of joke that made everyone laugh.

Humor is a powerful tool if you use it authentically. Be sure it isn't being used as a negative defense mechanism against real emotional pain for the sake of sparing embarrassment. It's always a good decision to be honest about your struggle. If you do feel embarrassed by your challenge, do well to admit it and then inject humor to take you out of this self-conscious emotion.

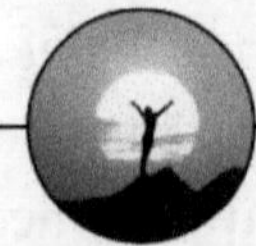

Special Notes about Humor

Humor plays an important accompanying role to moving through loss or transition.

Life is rarely as serious as we make it out to be. When you can master your fear of criticism, you bring light and hope to yourself and potentially to others.

It is up to you to laugh at situations, not in an effort to mask your pain, but to shine a light on your resilience.

When you can learn to laugh in the face of absurdity, major uncertainty becomes something with which you can more easily face.

Freeze Your Fear of What Others Might Think

The lady with the rice in her hair could have shot back angrily. Would a fear of social embarrassment from social criticism stop you from participating in life? If so, it may be time to freeze the fear.

When faced with a heavy challenge, it's easy to worry or fear how others will respond. For example, one private client of mine feared her mother's criticism if she were to fail at trying to nurse her soon-to-be first child. Her fear of criticism was so strong that she opted to feed her baby formula instead of trying to breastfeed. Although she believed breast milk is best, she allowed her fear of what someone else might say to influence her experience as a first-time mother.

This client came to me with regret about her last choice and was living in a state of inner disappointment for not having had the courage to face her fear of future criticism. She was seeking inner strength.

As a successful coaching client, she:

- Came to refocus her attention on her relationship with perfection and her connection to her fears;

- Learned to make clear-thinking and self-honoring decisions by making proactive choices.

You might not ever have to struggle to eat a fork full of rice. Then again, you might be caught in of fear of criticism from others. Make a choice to freeze your fear today and ignite independent choices to persevere.

Notes and Questions to Ask Yourself about Fear of Criticism

✎*Fear of embarrassment is a self-conscious emotional experience.*

Ask Yourself: Is a self-conscious mindset preventing you from making clear-thinking and self-honoring decisions?

✎*It can be stressful trying to ease someone's anger or attempts to judge you.*

✎*Humor is one expression of how you might embrace absurdity in uncertain, uncomfortable transitions.*

Ask Yourself: Am I willing to make a personal choice to embrace absurdity through challenges?

Habit #2A: Visual Trigger to Ignite Strong Habits

Light Up Weekly Intelligent Planning

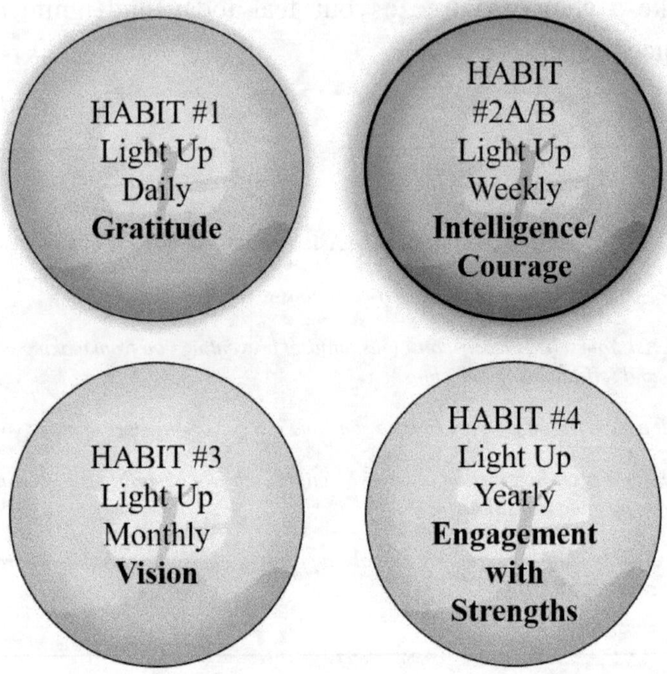

If a habit could talk, what might it say?

Habit #1Gratitude: For whom will I express gratitude today?

Habit #2A Intelligence: Whom will I seek to understand better this week as an intelligent solution to frustration?

Habit #2B Courage: Is my level of courage lower than I'd like it to be in my situation?

Habit #3 Vision: What is my vision of myself at the end of this month when it comes to my handling uncertainty?

Habit #4 Engagement with Strengths: What might I schedule on my birthday that helps me engage with my newfound and developing strengths?

Adapted from AMC Online Training in Perseverance Workshop

Second Level Perseverance-Habit #2A Intelligence*

Pyramid of Perseverance:
AMC Proactive Levels to Success™

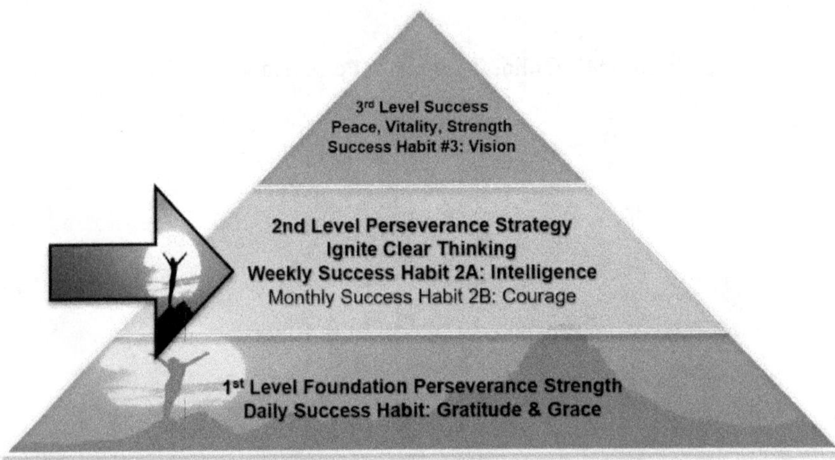

Proactive Life Mastery Academy™ Amy McCann Coaching™

CHAPTER 8
PREPARE TO IGNITE INTELLIGENT THINKING

A Meeting with Frustration

A park bench had never felt more uncomfortable on my rear. I had every choice to get up, but I felt frozen next the woman beside me. I shifted slightly, hoping she wouldn't notice how stiff I had become in response to her comment. It was one comment I heard repeatedly, and here it was again, greeting my ear like a fingernail scratch to a chalkboard. Shaking her head, she said, "I could never stay with my husband if something so bad happened."

I kept my peripheral vision locked on my twin daughters playing just feet away in a sandbox. Nodding my head, this woman didn't seem to have the sense that my eyebrows were now clenched tightly. Since I had heard this admission from several different women over many years, I started to develop the unfair conclusion that a lot of people suck when it comes to love, commitment, and strength. Talk about a paralyzing, judgmental mindset! What was I so upset about?

As we've discussed at length, conclusions can lead to bitterness. Still, was I justified in believing these women to be callous and selfish? Again, justifications are an example of a defensive mindset. The little girl fear in me could explain my defensiveness. Perhaps on some level, I was fighting against the fear that this many people could exist in the same mold as my father—people willing to bail out on their family in the face of hardship. It's a tidy psychoanalysis of things, but this isn't what was going on.

I was stuck in a closed mindset. It hadn't occurred to me to consider a struggle people might be dealing with—a real and scary fear of the unknown. I had succeeded in mentally connecting to potential struggles my father faced as a way to better understand his behavior to abandon his family. This was a gift of inner strength I built for myself. If I could do this with my father, I knew it was possible to drop my irritability with strangers and close friends alike.

With a beginner's mind I shed the assumption that people were callous. I started to look at my irritability more closely. I had been stuck trying to crack my own case of a fear of the unknown. I was fearful I might not be strong enough to handle one more disappointment in my situation. The only thing keeping me stuck was my imagination. In clearing my mind of irritable chatter, I realized I had moments when I imagined abandoning ship.

Wait a minute. How was imagining myself abandoning ship different from what these women were sharing? It was time to stop being so judgmental and set on a new path of understanding of myself and others.

Intelligent Choice to Understand

"Everything that irritates us about others can lead us to an understanding of ourselves."

~Carl Jung

A beginner's mind set me up for clear thinking. I came to better understand the power of our imaginations. I was trained in the use of my imagination my entire life in theatre. I experienced the magic –how it serves to bring dreams to life, ease pain, and motivate hopefulness. Now, I was reminded of the dark side of imagination. The side that screams scary voices inside your brain and shows moving pictures of failure crashing down upon your head.

My irritability with others had served a purpose. I came to understand how much I had allowed my imagination to extinguish my strengths. I came to understand others' responses by asking questions. I learned that there was in fact a fear of the unknown present for those I spoke with. In discussing it, I realized I had something to offer that could help others out of fear into a place of greater inner peace.

An exploration of irritability can lead to greater understanding of yourself. It is an intelligent choice to think like a beginner to better understand how your imagination might be holding you back. It's exciting to know we have power to change things just through the use of our minds.

Quick Check Intelligent Step: Understanding Others

Do I have irritability toward someone? Would I like to be less reactive and a more understanding person?

The fifth proactive habit in Stephen Covey's *The 7 Habits of Highly Successful People* is to understand first.

To help you move toward better understanding of others try saying these three words: *"Tell me more_______"*

Purpose: Exercises a beginner's mind
Objective: Shed assumptions

Proactive Life Mastery Academy™ Amy McCann Coaching™

Optimism, Grief, and Denial

Is there such a thing as over-inflated optimism in the face of uncertainty? I believe it is possible. Although I was connected to the Christopher and Dana Reeve story in a positive way, it changed a bit when I began experiencing ongoing disappointment. There was a period of time where I became hyper-focused on the good parts and their daily successes through struggle. I found it difficult to listen to the upsets and setbacks.

It was scary to face all that was lost as a couple. I avoided talking about my fears. I worked hard to stay optimistic. So, what's wrong with that, you might ask? The problem is that when you focus on optimism only, you close down any chance to grieve loss.

There is no doubt I was in touch with all that had changed. After all, I was in the thick of it. I was soldiering on. I just wasn't prepared for the grief process. I encourage you to explore your relationship with optimism in the face of overwhelming circumstances. Optimistic vision is important to your mental well-being. In my experience, this vision is best realized when you have dealt with grief.

Quick Card Check-In: Optimism-Grief-Denial

- Is it possible I am focused on positive things in an effort to avoid grieving?
- Do I believe I can handle talking about my feelings?
- Is there any loss I need to deal with and I'm too afraid to face?
- Is there a goal that no longer fits with my circumstance that I need to let go of?

Proactive Life Mastery Academy™ Amy McCann Coaching™

Prepare to Ignite Intelligent Planning

It's so great that you've come this far! Congratulations on practicing a weekly habit to create intelligent thinking through frustration.

Here's where we're going:

- Stories of courage, clear-thinking, and disappointment.
- A Life Performance Awareness Model™.
- My Top 7 Tips for Caregivers.

It takes intelligent planning and clear-thinking courage to imagine a vision of better days ahead when you are struggling through uncertainty.

Ask Yourself

Wouldn't it feel good to learn how to clear my mind of worry?

Wouldn't it feel great to hit a higher level of confidence in my daily life and relationships?

Six-Legged Drama: A Story of Clear Thinking

"You will come face to face with some scary things on your way to success. It helps to ignite a courageous mindset ahead of time. Simply winging it through life without any direction can set you back dramatically."

~Amy McCann

It was a six-legged dramatic scene backstage starring a New York City cockroach. The crusty creature was the size of a cigarette lighter. Its role was to choose a two-legged human in whom to ignite fear and light up a scream. I was the chosen human, perched on the landing of a staircase hidden behind the stage curtain.

I awaited my cue to enter stage left and participate in a dramatic play I had rehearsed for weeks. The rehearsal process is not a practice that tries to achieve perfectionist performance. Instead, it is a structured practice that opens the door to artistically imperfect, natural, and believable dialogue and emotion. To agree to show up ready to perform imperfectly takes courage. It is what actors do every day.

In my opinion, dramatic courage for an actor is the ability to:

- **Prepare** for the end goal/objective.
- **Embrace** uncertainty in meeting the objective.
- **Observe**, listen, and respond without judgment.
- **Improvise** as necessary to keep the show moving.
- **Let go** of the outcome (no attachment to applause or criticism).

My description of dramatic courage exercised by an actor (which is taught in the theatre) is similar to some major principles and habits taught by the world's leading self-development and success teachers. Personal development strategists tell us that goal setting (preparedness) and acceptance (embrace) of inevitable obstacles are central to success. A great deal of advice is given to watch for (observe) situations that are opportunities. Finally, the best personal and business coaches will guide you to detach yourself (let go) from any outcomes and focus on the process of working toward a vision.

Ask Yourself

What could happen if I learn to prepare for hardship?

What if I could learn to embrace absurdity in serious situations?

What if I were curious about how to actively observe as a way to stay calm?

What would it look like to improvise and let go of some things along the way?

A choice to practice any of these actions can help to remove a lot of worry. It ignites clarity in the face of ambiguity about where you're headed next. These are the things you should be rehearsing so that you aren't going through life winging it.

I was more prepared to meet this cockroach not because I had rehearsed a face-off. It was because I had been trained in the process of embracing uncertainty. I let go of the imaginary outcome that it might jump on my face. I chose to observe the critter briefly without judgment and to keep calm. I chanted inside my head, "It has a brown shell. It has long antennae." This observation allowed me to remain calm in my state of crawling skin. I needed to be present in order to hear my cue to enter the stage. My cue was heard, and the show went on, as did my high-performing ability to stifle a scream.

To help you perform at a higher level through uncertainty, feel free to participate in a life performance model on the next page.

Life Performance Awareness Model™

Performance in the Face of Uncertainty

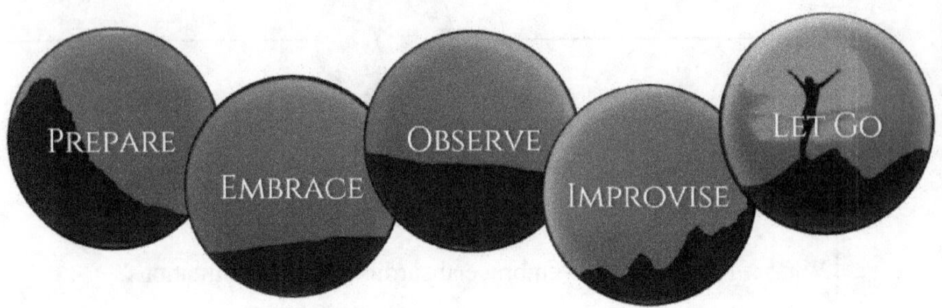

It's difficult to perform when you are feeling paralyzed by uncertainty. The purpose of this is to help you set a small goal and objective and improve your performance through awareness.

PREPARE: What three steps/tasks must I take to accomplish one challenging personal goal by Friday of this week?

EMBRACE: Using what I've learned about gratitude and grace, how could I better embrace uncertainty at work or home this week??

Do I need to improve this moving forward?

OBSERVE: What one person in my life or business will I commit to listening to this week? Am I prepared to observe rather than judge?

Do I need to improve this moving forward to improve my reactions and interactions?

IMPROVISE: If things don't go my way this week am I prepared to keep things moving in order to lower frustration and make progress?

If yes, how might I imagine improvising through a situation? If no, what action must I take to learn to improvise better?

LET GO: Do I have a difficult time letting go of the outcome of my objective or goal? If so, which devil might be behind it? (fear, doubt, disappointment, uncertainty)

Proactive Life Mastery Academy™ Amy McCann Coaching™

A Life Without a Plan

When caught in a real-life drama for which you didn't rehearse, you can be thrown hard off your stage. It pays to prepare yourself to respond better. Again, it's not about perfectionist rehearsals. It's about an agreement to commit to a process that takes some rehearsal. To wing it through life means you aren't fully participating in your present awareness or future vision for yourself

- **Loss of Direction:** Without structure, you lose direction in your love or business relationships. Even improvisation has a structure.
- **Communication Suffers:** If you haven't practiced listening, living in the moment, and improvising, communication with loved one's stinks.

- **Health is Compromised:** If you're too busy killing every last thing on your checklist, you risk a check-in to the hospital.
- **Reactive Behavior Becomes Your Theme:** An unstructured life is a reactive life.

Quick Card Check-In: Life Performance

Prepare: What goals and objectives have I prepared to help me prepare for the future?

Embrace: Do I embrace the possibility that things might not go my way?

Observe: Am I observing others or judging them?

Improvise: Am I willing to be flexible and improvise when things don't go my way?

Let Go: Am presently stressed because I'm worried about the outcome? If so, what area of life might improve if I were to let go of this worry?

Proactive Life Mastery Academy™ Amy McCann Coaching™

Dramatic Encounters: Courage to Weave a Different Story

The wings of a fly beat franticly. A sticky fate with a spider's web had been met. Much like a blood-sucking vampire, the owner of this web hid itself from daylight and was saving its prey for a midnight snack.

On this day, a knee-length skirt served nicely as a dark and cozy napping place for the web's owner. It took my sister Pam just one twirl of her skirt to awaken a wolf-like furry beast. This sent her into a blood-curdling scream. If this had been a cartoon, the mirror in front of which she was twirling would have surely cracked. Our newly built log cabin fit seven humans. Apparently, there was an arachnid realtor in town selling residency to hundreds of his large furry friends. It appeared our home was prime residency to these blood-thirsty beasts.

A favorite tale to recount involves my younger sister, Carol. Carol is our wittiest family member, and I dare say she can outwit anyone with humor. She is petite, shorter than I, and wears killer dimples when she smiles. She lives up to her fiery zodiac sign when she stands up for people. Back when we played in the piles of dirt that served double duty as a cat box, we played with miniature Lincoln Logs. We designed and built mini cabins, imagining which one we might want to live in.

After a challenging C-section delivery and giving birth to twins, it was Carol who was crouched beside the toilet in an effort to clean up bodily fluids. She was the one to come to my rescue in the most undignified position. All business, she wiped me clean, dressed me, and tucked me back into bed like a professional nurse. Later, I remarked that she was the most serious I had ever seen her. In her quick-witted way, she said, “Didn’t want you to split a stitch.”

My earliest and toughest memories are shared alongside Carol. She and I played in the egg-shaped mounds of dirt scattered about our property following the bulldozing of the burnt house. These mounds looked more like alien pods than heaps of earth and ashes. At times, I secretly wished a spaceship would swoop down and take me back to their planet, so I could escape mine. When I was through imagining such escape, my heart ached as a reminder to stay close to my family.

The summer following the fire, Carol and I kept busy outside, as evidenced by the dirt under our nails. We dug deep into the imaginary alien pod in hopes that we would uncover some toys that might have survived the fire and the harsh winter.

On other days, my sister and I had fun digging moats around mud castles. We giggled hysterically when our tiny white kitten Audrey squatted to take a poop in one of the rooms in a castle. It hadn't occurred to us that our playtime was unsanitary and that we were actually playing in a very large litter box. Fortunately, we survived.

In winter, the mounds of earth became prime real estate for sledding. Our screeches as we flew down the hill could be heard echoing off the mountains in the distance. Over and over, we crashed into one another. The snow sparkled like glitter beneath the moonlight. We eagerly dragged our sleds back up the hill for another crashing experience.

Back to my favorite tale about Carol. Picking up a slice of pizza from her paper plate was about to turn scary. Imagine this scene in slow motion. A slice of pizza, inches from my sister's lips. Eight furry legs dangle briefly, finishing with a wobbly landing onto an olive topping. My fiery younger sister hurls the pizza with the firmly attached spider to immediate death and destruction as it slams against a nearby wall.

My sister Pam's screams scared me most. To be fair, I had every reason to scream as well. After all, she and I were linked by a spider bite that had taken place a couple of years before in our farmhouse. As we awoke one morning, my eye and her lip had swollen to the size of golf balls. We were rushed to the hospital, where our wounds were drained.

Following the dress incident, I decided I didn't want to live in paralyzing fear of spiders. I needed to weave a different story for myself. As was usually the case, my imagination came to the rescue. One of my favorite stories is E.B. White's *Charlotte's Web*. I began to imagine these house spiders could talk and wondered what wisdom they might have to share. Although I didn't want to be their friends, I also didn't want to fear spiders the way my siblings did. Besides, I was immediately drawn to a natural purpose for being in our house. The nasty, annoying flies that made their way over from the farm next door were sure to meet their demise. No more buzzing in my ear to keep me awake at night.

Discovering a new mindset is like having a superpower. I've not been bothered by eight-legged creatures since then. It's a kind of reverse law of attraction. I seem to have effectively repelled them away from me.

Following my meeting with the armored insect in a backstage New York City theatre, I chose to maximize my power to remain calm should I ever come face to face with one again. It was during a family trip to Washington, D.C. that I chose to attend a cockroach petting session at a nearby museum. As the handler passed around these crusty creatures, I made a point to allow myself exactly five pets each.

~

The point of this story isn't to brag or impress you because I overcame some fears of pests. It isn't to encourage you to like spiders or pet a cockroach.

Here's my message:

- If you choose to approach fears more creatively or imaginatively, you have the advantage of living in a kind of mental harmony of which most people only dream of.
- You have the advantage of displaying a kind of courage that might inspire others (like your children).
- When you can dare to think differently, you can weave a new and more calming story for yourself to adjust a fearful mindset.

Let me know what superpower you discover as you learn to adopt a new mindset!

Courage to Face Disappointment

Many people have called me courageous over the years. While it's true that I've made some courageous decisions, I wasn't always able to maintain my courage in times of disappointment. Where had that brave little girl who faced spiders gone? I was now in my early twenties, face to face with disappointment and wrapped in mental anguish.

When I speak of courage, I mean my ability to find the harmony in my situation. This harmony could only be found through self-care. Following three years of burning disappointment, I became locked into a dead-end mindset as a result of extremely poor quality or huge gaps in home care services. I was counting on an entire home health industry to provide my boyfriend and me with some peace. This was my first mistake.

For the first three years, I was fit for the duties as a full-time caregiver to my boyfriend Kevin, who had been paralyzed as a quadriplegic. I was fit to try to be the best girlfriend I could be. I was fit to keep pressing on, still auditioning in the city, and following my dreams.

I worked a part-time job in the evenings following dinner and prior to the caregiving routine at night. I reignited a direct marketing sales business as a consultant as a way to allow a flexible work schedule around caregiving and auditioning.

At this three-year mark, we married. I was busy building leadership teams and earning free cruises for my husband and me.

Although I was struggling with bouts of depression accompanied by periods of worry, it seemed I had cracked the code on doing and having it all. As long as I was efficient and didn't give up, I felt successful. I hadn't yet realized that my definition of success was unhealthy.

I had no insight into what I was doing well and what I was doing less effectively. I had all the proof in the world that I could handle anything even on so few hours of sleep per night. This gave me some comfort in the face of inconsistent respite care. It gave me a false feeling of strength. Turns out that just because you can handle everything, doesn't mean it is good for you in the long term.

I was not on any mission to be a do-gooder model of strength. On the contrary, I was desperately hoping for a home health aide to rescue me from some of my daily responsibilities. It was not unreasonable to hope that one day we would finally catch a break if we fought hard enough.

What I experienced was paralyzing disappointment when it came to home care services. I felt we were in some kind of nightmare. I am not here to knock or dismiss the home health industry. I am referring to my personal experience during a very specific time of need in my life. Fortunately, we did hit upon an agency that succeeded in meeting the needs of our situation. Yours may not be such an arduous journey should you come to depend on these services.

Some Serious and Absurd Highlights in Home Care

Scary Trust Issues: The case of the missing Percocet. An agency investigation would solve the mystery.

Absurd Request: "Can you take care of my baby while I take care of your boyfriend?"

Absurd Greeting: "I'm here to take care of some guy."

The ability to inject humor into these situations was only the beginning. Humor served as a stress management tool, but I needed to enact some proactive steps in my relationship with disappointment. Since I was beginning to lose my faith, it was up to me to change my picture of my circumstance.

Awakening Discovery

I came to realize is that I was fighting for a life with Kevin that had already expired. I was working so hard to be a "normal" couple.

Although I can't speak for Kevin, I felt I was fighting for health care as much as I was hanging on to past hopes and dreams of the past. Why was I stuck on staying in the same spot when all signs pointed to a necessary shift away from how I was thinking, where I was living, and where my dreams were going?

I realized that my relationship with him was what mattered most. It wasn't a hard leap to begin imagining moving into another round of uncertainty if it meant I could feel more like a wife and less like a surviving caregiver. To help you see how my life was like back then, I share a window into the life I chose as a caregiver.

My Life as a Caregiving Girlfriend

Journaling has been an everyday habit of mine since the age of eight. As a caregiver, I experienced a rollercoaster ride of emotions and sought comfort in my daily journal entries.

When I look back on the early journal entries today, I see I was connected to my success in meeting daily responsibilities and to my emotional struggle. I had not a lot in the way of strategies to sustain my energy. A habit to think positively was scattered. Mostly, I was just good at pushing through. I was also becoming more bitter by the day as my life as a caregiving girlfriend started to take its toll. I loved my boyfriend, but I wasn't yet aware that I hadn't been loving myself very well. At the same time, the inability of the home health care agency to staff shifts was making me angry.

A Window into My Journal

(Reconstructed to fit our purposes)

Day One Survival Energy: The digital bedside clock reads 11:00p.m. The ringing in my ears feels sharp inside my skull as my body slumps between the sheets. I sigh in satisfaction of another efficient day under my belt. A lack of sleep could be to blame for the sharp ringing in my ears, but I press on. I have successfully completed tasks. A 9:00p.m. to 11:00p.m. caregiving routine that included full range of motion body exercises and various other tasks. My inner clock is programmed to awaken at 1:00a.m. and again at 3:00a.m. My body is trained for these interruptions in sleep. As a caregiver, it is a necessary interruption with the purpose to prevent bed sores—wounds that can occur when a person hasn't the ability to reposition his or her body.

Day Two Survival Perseverance: It's another day that begins at 5:00a.m. I'm glad I remembered to check to see that Kevin's wheelchair battery is fully charged. The cats did well to paw at my face to remind me of feeding time. Five hours of morning care routine accomplished! Some unexpected challenges arose, and things have settled now. I have to prepare breakfast today, but first, coffee! A drive to two doctor appointments is waiting on the other side of my morning oatmeal with bananas and raspberries. I love my life. I am persevering toward my goals and succeeding at meeting my responsibilities. Isn't this what perseverance is?

Day Three Disappointment Burns: Another hit of disappointment this week when another home health aide failed to show up. Ah! This roller coaster ride is getting old. My patience is waning. I sound like a wicked witch, and I feel like a monster. Have I managed to manifest a pointy hat and claws? It doesn't take much to see me go up in smoke as the days and nights seem to melt into one another. I have strong purpose every day, but is this who I've become?

Day Four Positive Thinking: I survived another stressful day. It's hard to concentrate on such little sleep. By midafternoon, I had to hustle to catch the mid-afternoon train into Manhattan. I was scheduled to audition for a four-part play series in Manhattan. Yay! A chance to work with seasoned professionals! Pouring over my play script was a challenge as the words seem to bleed together. I seem to keep reading the same paragraph over and over no matter what I read. A feeling of irritation boiled while on the train. I'm sick of these irritable moments rearing their ugly head! One thought did interrupt. It said, "Use your irritable mood to inform the role you are about to play." Isn't this what they call positive thinking?

Day Five Wonder Woman Success: Throughout the day, I was able to accomplish the one hundred and twenty things on my list. Yippee for me! I even had a chance to volunteer at the local animal shelter for few hours. I feel energetic despite my lack of sleep. Pouring the fifth cup of coffee must have made up for lost shut eye. I'm pushing through. I'm persevering. Some days I'm depressed. Thankfully, today is not one of those days. Today, I feel like Wonder Woman. After all, I've kept most of this up for a few years and haven't collapsed yet! Isn't this success?

Day Six Pity Party: I hear the seething sound of bitterness seep into my language. A self-pity party erupts more frequently than I'd like. I should try to schedule these sessions. I feel no one understands the struggles I go through. Am I making things look too easy? After all, I have met my goal to achieve as close to normal a life as before Kevin's paralysis. I show up at events even if they are at 11:00a.m. and include a two-hour drive to get there. No one knows the amount of sleep sacrifice that goes into attending a celebratory event. Neighbors wonder how I'm doing it all and even call me a kind of super woman, but I know the truth. I'm no Wonder Woman or Super Woman. I am cracking under the surface. I'm paranoid I might collapse today. Great, now I feel guilty! Oh, woe is me. What is wrong with me? Snap out of it! How can I feel so badly when Kevin's issues are so much more challenging?

Day Seven Sacrifice: You'd think I'd learn. I once again succeeded at attending a family event. Now I am paying the price for sacrificing my sleep. I feel a sore throat coming on. Time to crash into bed. I think it is time I was honest about how much trying to live a normal life is costing me. I know I have to start saying no to some things. How can I learn to say no to events? Is saying no my only option?

Comparing Struggles May Not Be Helpful

Day Six Reflection: Remember, we are here to make struggle connections as a helpful way to make progress. You must be careful not to compare your struggle as if yours isn't worthy of examining. There will always be someone to whom you can point who has it worse.

Quick Card Check-In: Guilt

If you perceive someone's struggle as worse than your own, guilt can set in.

How do you know if your struggle is worth attending to? Here is one way to know if your struggle is worth some attention and remove your guilt!

Is my struggle negatively impacting my ability to think straight?

Is my struggle bringing forth bad thoughts about myself?

Is my struggle negatively impacting your relationships?

If you answer yes to even one, isn't it worth attending to your struggle?

Proactive Life Mastery Academy™ Amy McCann Coaching™

My Top 7 Tips to Become a Healthy Caregiver:

- **Be Aware:** I wasn't aware that my negative relationship with ongoing disappointments was causing stress.
- **Avoid Denial:** I wasn't aware I was in a denial stage of grief, which added to my frustration and magnified all that was negative.
- **Be Mindful of Your Stress Response:** I wasn't mindful of my type of fighting stress response.
- **Be Connected to Your Overall Wellbeing:** I wasn't connected to my emotional wellbeing.
- **Consider the Consequences of Pushing Forward:** I didn't consider the consequences of pushing forward to fit back into a life that no longer existed. Ask yourself why you're pushing forward and if it is worth it to your health? Make a choice to flow forward instead with honesty and focus on assistance rather than disappointment.
- **Gain New Insights:** I had no insight into my healthy vs. non-healthy perseverance habits.
- **Be Clear on a Vision for Yourself:** I had no vision into my future goals because I was so busy fighting in the present. Work to create a clear vision of where you are going.

Not following these guidelines can lead to chronic stress and some form of resentment.

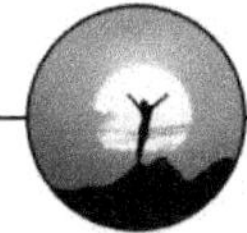

My Thought for the Day

"You can only give more steady attention to another's health if you care to give more steady attention to your health first."

~Amy McCann

Mistakes to Avoid in the Face of Disappointment

- Sitting in struggle too long
- Waiting for that lesson to magically appear and reveal itself
- Waiting for prayers to be answered, and when they aren't, creating more internal disappointment for yourself
- Wanting someone in the world to help support you in your time of disappointment, and when they don't appear, prolonging your time with disappointment

I hope to have succeeded in inspiring you to believe that you are not here to carry the weight of the world on your shoulders. Your struggle does matter, and that you are not alone.

CHAPTER 9
CLEAR-THINKING CONFIDENCE AND COURAGE

Confidence in New Beginnings

Four words sparked a higher-level commitment to a relationship: It's a new beginning. Now it was time to begin a higher-level commitment to my health. This time, I was looking forward, not simply pushing forward.

Connect with Your Foundation

"How much more do you have to go through before you're considered strong?" Awaiting a ride to the airport, my best friend since kindergarten sat slouched in the corner of my sectional style couch in my New Jersey condominium. It was an appropriate question given my life's story.

Today, Susan is still my best friend, a successful mother of three, a loyal wife to her husband, and a professional romance writer. She posed this question on the heels of my boyfriend's injury.

We both laughed in resignation to life's uncertain plans. We knew the truth. Life can be cruel in its effort to make you stronger while at the same time not killing you. It seemed there was no real point in trying to find the point in things. We weren't cynical, just realistic to life's disappointments. We were twenty-three years old and sitting on a nineteen-year friendship.

One more thing Susan said that hit home: “Make sure you take care of yourself. I don’t want to have to come and rescue you.” It was a new beginning of understanding just how important that statement was. I would soon have no choice but to recognize that I was running out of caregiving steam.

I was living in a wheelchair-accessible residence. How I came to find it was another example of good fortune. In a phone book search for a local realtor, something attracted me to call one agency above the others. A man on the other end of the line greeted me, and I explained my urgent need to find wheelchair-accessible housing.

“You’re in luck,” the man said. After a slight pause, he continued, “I happen to be the only realtor I know of in the area who sits in a wheelchair. Finding accessible housing is my specialty.” Was this a coincidence or a blessing? I choose to add it to my foundation of good fortune timing that showed up in times of great uncertainty.

In large part, the reason for my courage and strength today was sitting across from me on my couch that day. This five-foot blonde with a very loud voice was the foundation of what had kept my pyramid of perseverance standing. At age four, our purpose had been built to be there for each other. By the time we were teens, we were official blood sisters. We had each pricked a finger and rubbed them together in commitment to our sisterly friendship. Since then, my best friend has proven to be the most loyal person I could have ever wished for. We seemed to have figured out the harmony in a relationship.

Foundation of Friendship Ignites Lifetime Confidence

Who in your life has lit up your confidence? How often do you think about this person?

Following the structure of what we're learning, I want to break down how my best friend Susan contributed to our cherished friendship. She is a model example of how to achieve personal success in relationships. It takes acts, not thought, to nourish any relationship.

Acts of Gratitude

Susan has spent forty years actively honoring me as her friend. Two acts of gratitude that stand out are a handmade photo album of our friendship along with personal poems as a wedding gift to my husband and me and naming her first- and only-born daughter after me.

Acts of Courage

Susan takes regular action to include me in things that will test my confidence and courage. She is literally the friend who pushes you down a ski slope after teaching you the rules. She allows no time for hesitation and sets you up to achieve. She is a master at doling out challenges with your best interest at heart.

She has helped me achieve a more courageous mindset by:

- Believing in my power to influence others to lead themselves;
- Cracking the whip anytime she smells a hint of self-sabotage;
- Unsticking my thoughts when I get analysis paralysis so that I will take the next step.

Acts of Harmony/Peace/Perseverance/Success

Achieving harmony means telling yourself the truth first. In times when I was not handling things well, I sometimes appeared with my shiny mask smile. Susan was the only one to see through it.

Are there times in your life you could do better to shed a false mask? What are the benefits of telling the truth about how you feel?

I learned how to be more peaceful with myself by admitting I was struggling. Susan made me see that the lies I told myself were as damaging as any lie I could tell anyone else.

As the flames consumed our farmhouse so many years ago, it was Susan who stood by me shortly after my brother was transported to the hospital. She told me not to worry—my birthday party could be held at her house that year. Her dad served on the fire department and helped put out the flames. Unfortunately, they weren't able to save the house, as the gas tanks blew prior to the fire department arriving.

One year, we attended a Women Inspiring Women Event together here in New Hampshire. Jack Canfield was the speaker. When he asked us to turn to the person beside us and say what we appreciate about them, we were both speechless.

Tears streamed down Susan's cheeks, and I felt a lump in my throat. Too many memories and too many moments of appreciation to count. Silence seemed to fit in that moment. Now, I've created a system that honors her, and you can do the same for your friends, too. I hope this book speaks loudly and clearly to my ongoing appreciation of her.

Fearful and Focused Persistence

One of the core lessons in courage that I gained from my best friend is to sit with fear yet stay focused. By this, I mean the ability to acknowledge fear in situations and succeed through with focused attention to come out the other side. As if she weren't accomplished enough, Susan is an Army veteran. I'll never forget the video she shared of her making it through the tear spray test.

An unattractive scene of snot hanging from her nose to her feet is not something you see every day. She made it through the obstacle course with her eyes sealed shut without collapsing. It was a full demonstration of Susan's fearful and focused attitude in approaching all sorts of things in life.

I've learned for myself that it is possible to be fearful and still maintain focus. This is what mental strength is. I'll never forget the time Susan gave me skiing instructions. She then swiftly pushed me down the mountain before I could wimp out. We were just nine years old, and she taught me how to focus in the face of fear of making it down the mountain alive.

Fearless and Foolish Persistence

To demonstrate fearless foolishness is to ignore oncoming fire of uncertainty and to attempt to dance around it. When the fire of uncertainty is close, it is okay to be fearful. It is wise to stay focused on the direction in which direction the flames are blowing. It takes courage to blow them in a new direction to avoid getting burned.

That Which Does Not Kill You Can Still Make You Collapse: A Reflection

Years after that grave day in the Canadian hospital, I was busy applying my mascara. I felt a stampede of horses beat about my chest. As faintness set in, the mascara wand landed firmly into my tear duct. "I'm strong," I told myself. My efforts to clear the black smear from my eyeball just seemed to make my heart race faster. I assured myself aloud that I just need to breathe. "Maybe I'm dehydrated," I thought. "No, this is very, very wrong," I feared.

Next, I was staring at a flickering fluorescent light hovering above my head. With each flicker of light, a voice within me screamed, "You're not a cat! You don't have nine lives, stupid! You are not built to chase! You are not the energizer bunny with ever-lasting batteries!"

Call it God, my guardian angel, the Universe. This undeniably powerful voice was fed up with my go-it-alone mindset, and my body was angry with me. My thoughts were interrupted. “September?” a loud male voice echoed off the walls. It was a nurse asking me to confirm the birth month typed on the hospital bracelet. After my nod of confirmation, he announced that I was ready to be admitted as an overnight patient for observation.

I was persevering insofar as I wasn’t dead yet. My creative thinking wings were trapped. I needed out of this mind web and into a clear-thinking space. It was time to grow a new relationship with disappointment.

Where was I to begin? It turns out I needed the courage to commit in a way I hadn’t before. I needed to begin my strength from a place of greater self-love. I needed to commit to self-care.

STRESS & SELF-CARE AWARENESS EXERCISE

How Aware Are You?

Questions to Contemplate:

How often do I lack self-confidence in how I can handle things?

- ☐ Every day
- ☐ Every week
- ☐ Frequent
- ☐ Once in a while

Do I find myself prone to hiding or running away from others when I doubt myself?

- ☐ Every day
- ☐ Every week
- ☐ Frequent
- ☐ Once in a while

Do I depend on others to fulfill my happiness because of self-doubt about my own ability to be happy?

☐ Yes ☐ No

Is the way I'm doing things now the most effective way to serve myself and others?

☐ Yes ☐ No

Where on the scale do you place your awareness of your relationship with stress response and self-care?

←——————————————————————→

Not That Aware | Somewhat Aware | Getting Fully Aware

Adapted from Proactive Life Matters Academy™ Online Training in Perseverance
Personal Commitments Guide to Success Worksheet

Designed by, Amy McCann Coaching™

Extinguish Perfectionist Thinking

I wanted a perfect ending. Now I've learned the hard way that some poems don't rhyme, and some stories don't have a clear beginning, middle, and end. Life is about not knowing, having to change, taking the moment, and making the best of it without knowing what's going to happen next. Delicious ambiguity.

~Gilda Radner, American writer, actor, & comedian

Self-care can come in many forms. A belief in your ability to handle a situation can be considered one form of self-care. What happens when you are trying so hard to get things right only to be left disappointed by your efforts?

When anything we face leads to an ambiguous outcome, we may stress from a feeling of failure. A perfectionist attitude to force uncertainty to make sense is a recipe for self-doubt and disappointment. Why not begin today to retire this mindset and choose a beginner's mind moving forward?

Quick Card-Check-In: Stress & Self-Care

Do I feel confident I can handle things this week?

If not, is it because I fear something? If so, what is it?

Is it because I am doubtful of my capabilities? If so, what action could I take to bring back confidence?

Do I feel paralyzed by uncertainty of my situation?

Have I been running away from potential disappointment? If so, what is scaring me the most?

If I keep going like this, who might this effect negatively?

Proactive Life Mastery Academy™ Amy McCann Coaching™

Inner Strengths Journey: Mindful Perseverance

One day while journaling for more than an hour, a light bulb went off. How was I able to do so much for so long? I loved my boyfriend. I was committed in my duties. I could execute getting things done. I was persistent. So, why wasn't this enough to keep me healthy?

I discovered some reasons why I wasn't persevering so well. Below, I've summarized and categorized them into the types of persevering strengths I defined in Chapter 1. This will help you discover some of your own reasons behind why you might be wearing yourself down.

> **Emotional:** In an effort to push forward, I hadn't allowed myself to feel the emotional grief associated with all the losses we had experienced as a couple. I kept waiting for circumstances and my boyfriend to lighten my emotional load of suppressing grief, fatigue, and disappointment.

Your Turn to Ask Yourself: Am I putting my happiness in others' hands?

Mindset: I allowed disappointment in home health services to give birth to an isolating and fixed mindset that no help was available.

Your Turn to Ask Yourself: Am I presently in a fixed mindset that has me believing I am the only one responsible for all things in my situation?

Survival: Efficiency style habits kept me feeling like I was surviving instead of creating a thriving lifestyle. While I succeeded in my responsibilities, I was also slowing burning out. Survival mode prevented me from igniting a long-term vision

Your Turn to Ask Yourself: Am I busy surviving a TGIF lifestyle? Could a long-term vision create a more meaningful daily experience?

Spiritual: Once I lost my beginner's mind, I was unable to breathe.

Your Turn to Ask Yourself: Am I spiritually disconnected from my inner strengths and faith?

Power to Choose: I realized I was choosing daily responsibilities above my power to choose to care about my health.

Your Turn to Ask Yourself: I know it's important to complete my daily responsibilities, but am I also neglecting my health?

Daily Strength: I realized I hadn't had the courage to communicate my inner struggles. I believe now that I was in a denial phase of grief that I could not identify back then. I was frozen in my ability to express myself in a healthy way.

Your Turn to Ask Yourself: Am I out of touch with my emotions? Do I find myself emotionally exploding, running away, or freezing up when it comes to communication?

Physical Strength: It was obvious I hadn't been checking in with the signs of stress. My body let me know in the harshest way that it was done with my ignoring ways.

Your Turn to Ask Yourself: Am I checking in with physical symptoms to see if I've been neglecting my physical strength?

*Adapted from Proactive Life Matters Academy™ Online Training in Perseverance
Personal Commitments Guide to Success Worksheet
Designed by, Amy McCann Coaching™

Now It's Your Turn

On the next page, take a moment to ignite the courage to commit to your self-care. A choice to commit to your health and success is confidence.

Consider this your Proactive Method of Stress Reduction.

Quick Card Anytime Check-In: Lifelong Strengths
A Mindful Perseverance Exercise

Emotional: Am I putting my happiness in others' hands?

Mindset: Do I believe I am the only one responsible for my situation?

Survival: Do I feel like I'm surviving through the week, or thriving?

Spiritual: Am I disconnected from deep breathing and faith?

Power to Choose: Can I choose to focus on my health today, or am I choosing to focus on doubts about the future, or disappointments of the past?

Daily Strength: Are my daily emotions depleting my energy?

Physical Strength: Have I checked in with my physical symptoms lately? Could my symptoms be due to stress?

Designed by, Amy McCann Coaching™

Habit #2B: Visual Trigger to Ignite Strong Habits

Light Up Weekly Courage

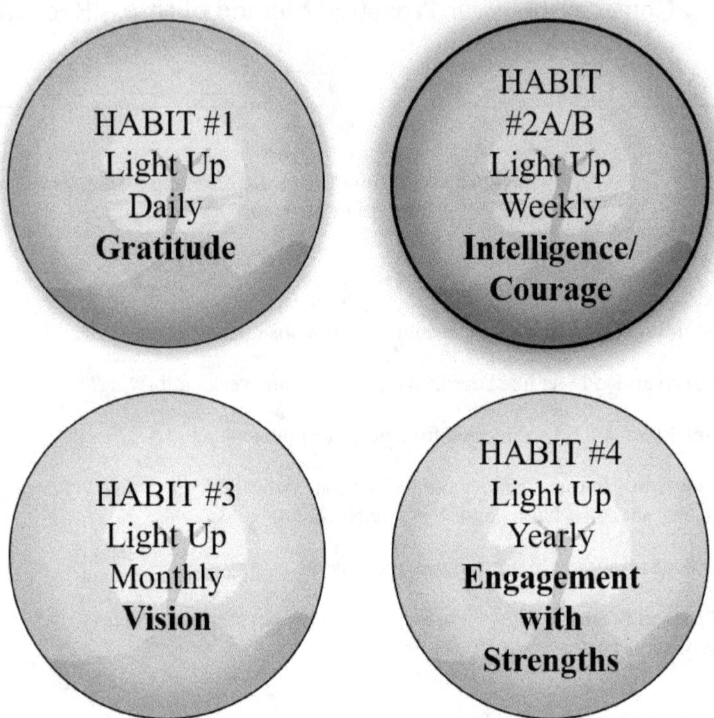

*Adapted from Proactive Life Mastery Academy™ Online Training in Perseverance

Second-Level Perseverance-Habit #2BCourage

Pyramid of Perseverance:
AMC Proactive Levels to Success™

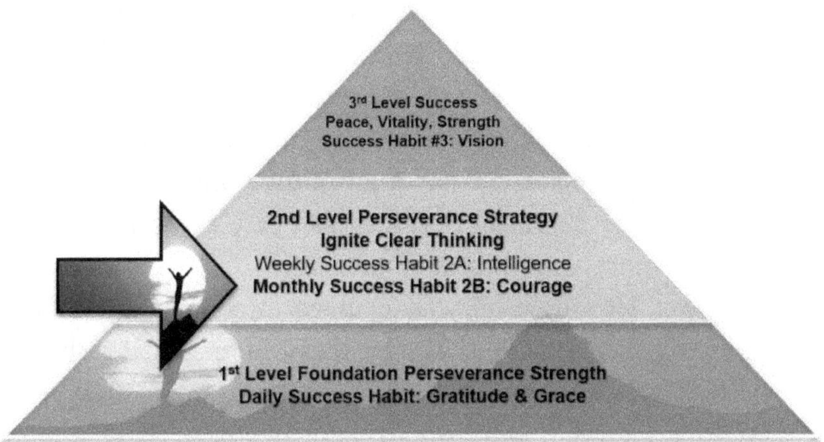

Adapted from Proactive Life Matters Academy™ Online Training in Perseverance
Personal Commitments Guide to Success Worksheet
Designed by, Amy McCann Coaching™

Commitment Takes Courage

> *"It is easy to live for others. Everybody does. I call on you to live for yourself."*
>
> *~Ralph Waldo Emerson*

Although love was the greatest driving force in my commitment and dedication to take on such a big responsibility, it took a deeper kind of love for myself to create the beautiful life I imagined I, and we, could have.

When you are facing a tough transition, nothing you've learned so far will stick for the long-term if you are lacking one important thing: a full commitment to yourself. By this, I mean a conscious and intentional commitment to care about your emotional, physical, mental, and spiritual wellbeing.

Love for another person isn't enough to keep you healthy. I would argue I love my children more than any person on this planet. However, that kind of deep love can't be expressed well or experienced fully if I've forgotten how to love myself first.

I will share with you the major mistakes I made, the successes I discovered, and how I came to learn the difference between healthy and unhealthy perseverance as a full-time primary caregiver. While your life may be vastly different, self-care and self-love should be your foremost commitment to yourself.

Next, let's light up your courage to commit to yourself. Let's agree to have the courage to step away from a society that preaches success as some kind of product that comes out of depleting self-sacrifice and grit. Let's work to energize you.

If you want to be personally successful in your relationships and business, choose to sacrifice things that no longer make sense. Be brave to repurpose your commitments.

HABIT #2A/B: INTELLIGENT PLANNING/ COURAGE STATEMENT WORKSHEET*

I understand that courage is necessary if I want to succeed in the face of uncertainty. Here, I am exercising the courage to stand up for my health above all else. I am choosing to become more aware of my courage when it comes to the uncertainty fear, doubt, and disappointment. I am choosing to act with courage to fulfill a goal to improve my mental, physical, spiritual, and emotional strength.

Week One Ignite and Recite: Courage Awareness

Today I feel________________ when I think of my level of courage in the face of uncertainty.

Yesterday I felt ________________ about my level of courage in the face of fear.

Last week I acted with courage to ___________________ so that I could improve ______________,

I learned this about myself: ____________________________

____.

____.

____.

To express my courage this week, I will take the following action in one of these following areas: mental health/physical health/spiritual health/emotional health. ______________________________

____.

____.

Week Two Ignite: Mindfulness

Because I expressed my courage last week, I have found that I now feel ____.

____.

____.

Repeat this process moving forward.

Adapted from Proactive Life Matters Academy™ Online Training in Perseverance
Adapted From: AMC Personal Commitments Guide to Success Worksheet Designed by Amy McCann Coaching™. To receive a FREE copy of the full guide, email: amy@3DStressSolutionsCoach.com. Type "AMC Commitments" in the subject line.

HABIT #2B: IGNITE WEEKLY COURAGE WORKSHEET

A Balanced Self-Care Guide

Through awareness and courageous action, how do I choose to improve my relationships, work life, business endeavors, or dreams?

1) Relationships

What do I feel most uncertain, doubtful, disappointed, or fearful about this week when it comes to my relationship with?

What is one act of emotional courage I can take to diminish or extinguish my uncertainty, fear, doubt, or disappointment that will improve my relationship with this person?

2) Work Life

What do I feel most uncertain, doubtful, disappointed, or fearful about when it comes to my role at work?

What is an act of mindset courage I can take to diminish or extinguish my uncertainty, fear, doubt, or disappointment that will improve my confidence in my role at work?

3) Business Endeavor/Dream

What do I feel most uncertain, doubtful, disappointed, or fearful about when it comes to my business venture or dream?

What act of persevering courage can I take to ignite my energy?

Confidence Awareness Measure*

Using the confidence scale, how confident do you feel about keeping a commitment to yourself for at least a week?

Cold with Confidence | Warm with Confidence | Hot with Confidence

Despite your level of confidence, do you feel that self-care is an important element of success?

☐ Yes ☐ No

Adapted From: Proactive Life Mastery Academy™
Designed by Amy McCann Coaching™.

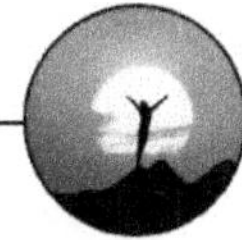

Quick Card Weekly Check-In: Courage

How do I exercise emotional, mindset, and persevering courage this week?

Day 1:____

Day 2:____

Day 3:____

Example: To exercise my emotional courage (EC) I will admit to my wife that I am fearful of this next stage of life

Example persevering courage: I agree to stick to my commitment to meet with my financial advisor to face my fear of future financial instability

EC=Emotional Courage
MC=Mindset Courage
PC=Persevering Courage

Proactive Life Mastery Academy™ Amy McCann Coaching™

CHAPTER 10
COURAGEOUS BELIEFS

In the previous chapter, you practiced a courageous commitment to self-care. It also takes courage to shift your mindset from doubtful to confident in your ability to face daily life challenges and tough times.

A Courageous Mind Shift Belief About Stress

PRESENT BELIEF:

I'm so stressed out!

MIND SHIFT BELIEF and AFFIRMATION:

I am not obligated to be stressed!

A Courageous Mind Shift Belief About Purpose

PRESENT BELIEF:

I have no idea what my purpose is.

MIND SHIFT BELIEF and AFFIRMATION:

Today, and every day, my purpose is to live in a foundation of gratitude, grace, and faith instead of worry, fear, and anxiety.

Once you can adopt this as your most important daily mindset, you will breathe a bit easier. Please keep this one sentence with you the next time you're tempted to overreact to something.

Worry Due to Prolonged Survival Thinking

There are circumstances of uncertainty where you are required to initiate, exercise, and endure some survival steps of adjustment. We all expect to endure some sleepless nights when agreeing to take on the uncertain role of parenting, for example. It does help to prepare for help along the way so you don't burn out. Here, I want to help you prevent paralyzing worry as a result of surviving through good as well as tough times and prepare to take care of yourself.

In the parenting example, to be proactive is not to simply prepare a baby's room. It means building in a self-care plan prior to the baby being born. To me, this is the most effective form of parenting. Proactive efforts remove the kind of paralyzing worry and emotional and physical depletion we might otherwise suffer. Self-care takes you out of survival steps and onto a confident stage where you can perform your duties well, even when things get dramatic.

In more long-term circumstances of uncertainty, responsibilities can leave us stuck in survival mode beyond the initial stages of adjustment. Here is where I want you to pay close attention. If you are suddenly hit with caring for a parent, for example, a survival step might require you to move your parent from his or her residence into a care facility. Yes, there is some stress involved, and this is where your survival skills will carry you through.

If you haven't done any personal development work before this new stage or transition in life, your survival skills will burn out eventually. To hold true to your responsibilities is to hold true to your personal commitment in self-care beyond the survival stage. If you've never made a commitment to yourself, now is the time.

Fiery Four Devils Examined: Student Feedback

Fiery Devil #1: Uncertainty is my devil when it comes to self-care.

Type of Stress Response Associated

Flight

Stressful Worry Associated

What if I finally step away to take care of myself and something bad happens? I could never forgive myself.

Mindset about Self-Care

I care about myself, I just know now is not the right time.

Fiery Devil #2: Fear

Type of Stress Response Associated:

Flight

Stressful Worry Associated:

What if I let my guard down to trust someone and find out I was wrong that they could do the job well?

Mindset about Self-Care:

If I take care of myself, I am taking a big risk. It's scary to leave my responsibilities in the hands of others. I like to feel in control.

Fiery Devil #3: Doubt

Type of Stress Response Associated:

Freeze (I feel stuck)

Stressful Worry Associated:

I'm most worried that there's simply no time when it comes to my situation to really be able to care for myself properly.

Mindset about Self-Care:

Self-care is a kind of luxury, I think. I doubt anyone has enough time to consistently take care of themselves in this hectic society.

Fiery Devil #4: Disappointment

Type of Stress Response Associated:

Fight

I've seen how things go as soon as I take a moment to myself. I can't count on anyone to help out, and my family gives me a guilt trip when I even think about doing something I want to do.

Stressful Worry Associated:

I worry I'm not as important to my family as they are to me.

Mindset about Self-Care:

Maybe my friends are right to say that being a parent is hard work and the breaks don't come until they are out on their own.

SELF-EMPOWERMENT AWARENESS EXERCISE

When it comes to uncertainty, how confident do I feel at this point about my ability to empower myself with grace, intelligent thinking, and courage on a daily and weekly basis?

Cold with Confidence   Warm with Confidence   Hot with Confidence

Despite the level of confidence in yourself, do you feel that self-empowering habits, behaviors, and actions are an important to overall success?

- ☐ Yes
- ☐ No
- ☐ Not sure yet

Proactive Life Mastery Academy™ Amy McCann Coaching™

PART II SUMMARY

Congratulations! Part II is complete! You've accomplished the following intelligent actions to ignite peace:

- ✓ Explored the Consequences of Stress
- ✓ Completed Inner Strengths Journey
- ✓ Fastened Proactive Building Block #2: Courage
- ✓ Participated in a Balanced Weekly Self-Care Exercise
- ✓ Committed to Weekly Courage Action Steps
- ✓ Gained Confidence Awareness
- ✓ Completed Daily Mindset Shifts
- ✓ Learned About the Consequence of Worry

Drink In Your Progress

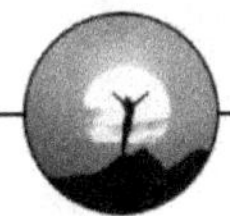

Action Step

Drink a glass of water to keep your body hydrated.

Suggested Options:

To Relieve Anxiety: enjoy a cup of peppermint tea
To Boost Energy: enjoy a cup of green tea

PART III
PERSONAL SUCCESS THROUGH UNCERTAINTY

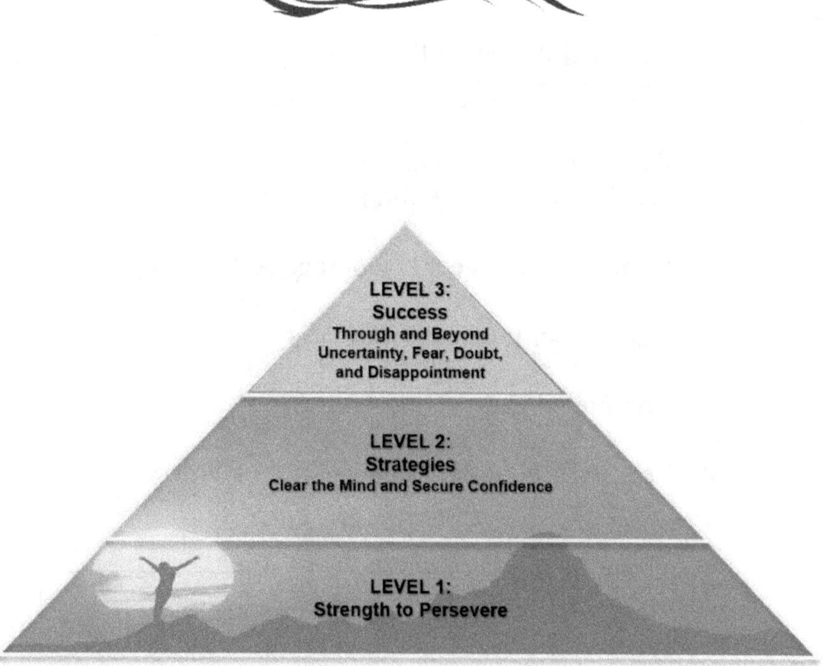

CHAPTER 11
FINAL ENDINGS AND REDEFINING STRENGTH

Life Goes On: A Story of Strength and Letting Go

It was coincidence that my brother began dating Janet around the same time my boyfriend and I started dating. It was three years prior to my boyfriend's spinal cord injury the first time I met her. I couldn't help but admire Janet's tall, hourglass physique and the way her curly brown hair bounced. She happened to be a single mother of a teenage girl whom we immediately adored. My brother would come to help to raise her as his stepdaughter.

One sunny afternoon, I reached for my ringing phone. "Hi, Amy! It's Janet. Are you busy? Um, I was wondering…?" Janet paused as if to cue me, and I obliged by asking in curiosity, "Yes?" After another pause, she continued, "Could you be the designer of your brother's and my wedding?" Of course, I accepted her invitation. We were off to plan a very simple backyard wedding that included a local band, a large rented tent, and champagne. I was honored that she also agreed to be the flower designer for my wedding.

A year later, we went on to celebrate a double honeymoon Caribbean cruise. I'm certain I manifested material good fortune when I landed a very large cash bingo win. To our excitement, it closely covered the cost of both our trips. As I lay the cash out in one of our cabins, Janet cupped her mouth with both hands, and tears streamed down her face. "I, I still can't believe you won! It's amazing!"

The moment B-12 was called back at the third level of the ship's theatre, Janet's brown curls bounced in unison with her jump out of a chair. She helped to carefully stuff my winnings in my bra on our trek back to my cabin. There's nothing quite like a herd of strangers yelling in your face "Congratulations!" as a boatload of cash winnings spills out of cleavage. The entire week of the cruise, I insisted that I would be the final winner on our last sailing night. It was a kind of strong knowing I've felt about other things in my life. I was so confident I would win, I promised to purchase a bottle of champagne to celebrate. I believe these moments of clarity and reward come when I've aligned myself to mentally relax and be open to possibilities.

As life goes on, we can choose to connect the dots to people who've made a difference in our path and in how our perceptions might have been shaped. Janet is the person I viewed as my closest confidant when it came to some deep hurts I'd experienced. She is the one who moved me into a new understanding of strength when dealing with one certainty in life we must all face.

A Time of Certainty and Uncertain Strength

It was three decades since the day I struggled to see past elbows and waists of adults. A vision of my brother on his worst day and a moment crouched in the ashes were a distant memory now.

On this day, perched on a stool was my sister-in-law Janet. She requested that I be her hairdresser that morning. She wanted a more comfortable, easy-to-care-for hairstyle. With each bit of trim, Janet exclaimed, "I feel lighter!" I felt heavy with emotion as each of the brown curls I admired dropped to the floor, each with one final bounce.

It was a day when certainty became my devil. As the permanency of death loomed, uncertainty now seemed the lesser of two evils to deal with. It was a burning reality to know we were all close to losing such a beautiful person. As I moved a facecloth down along her long, sleek arm, I took notice of the rosy colored nail polish she chose to keep her hands looking pretty. Gone now were her pretty curls, yet she still held up as one of the prettiest faces I had grown to know. After a bed bath, she brought the soft sheet to her chin. Her eyes closed and took her into a restful nap before my brother was to return.

The question we all ask rattled in my brain: Why another round of terrible suffering?

Once again, my brother was the shining example of perseverance rather than victimhood. His compassionate dedication stepped in, allowing him to take care of his wife from beginning to end.

Janet and I had grown close in our discussions about life struggles. We supported each other's pursuits in home business ventures. She was adventurous in exploring many hobbies and enrolling herself in interesting classes. Janet tried and accomplished many things, and we often joked that she lived many lives.

In addition to her curiosity, one of Janet's gifts to the family was her many personal creations. Her creative spirit lives on in the homes of each family member in the form of personalized Christmas stockings and pillows. She crafted homemade stuffed animals for my newborn twins that still sit at the ends of their beds as teenagers. Janet and I exchanged letters over the years, and I have kept all of them. Each was as thoughtfully inquisitive as it was updating.

Now, as I stroked her smooth head gently, it took me everything I had to hold back my tears. It wasn't that I believed this made me appear strong. In her sweet way Janet asked, "Um, would you mind not crying at my funeral?" I recall the sting I felt in my chest. She was accepting of her fate and called upon me to do something I wasn't certain I could fulfill. On another day, she said, "I'm counting on you to be the strong one." What did she mean, strong one? Did it matter? I decided it didn't and made my promise to be strong in the way she chose to define it.

Once again, I was experiencing emotional pain and the peripheral pain of others who were experiencing great loss. The pain my brother must have been experiencing seemed palpable to me.

I felt honored that my brother asked me to speak at Janet's memorial service. I remembered her words: "I expect you to be the strong one." If her definition of strong was to hold back tears, then I needed to honor it. I needed to remove any fears or nervousness I had that family members or strangers might judge me. I managed to hold it together for Janet's sake. It is not my business to know if anyone present noticed or cared about my tearless display to privately honoring my sister-in-law.

Janet brought light and humor to her own memorial service. She added her quirky spirit to the mix that day as the reverend shared that Janet had joked to have Michael Jackson's *Thriller* played.

I found a kind of peace with Janet during her time of illness. It was as if she lifted me to another level of strength by holding me accountable to stay strong. In some small way, she asked me to add light to this permanent last page of her life. I was influenced to leave my self-consciousness behind and honor her the way she wished. Holding back tears for that short time allowed me to shine a light on some humorous memories I had of her. Hopefully I did well to honor her spirit in the way she wanted. In some small way, I hope it served to bring comfort to my brother.

How I Believe This Story Can Help

The act of honoring others' wishes can be difficult. A choice to show up differently from how others expect you should might compromise how they perceive you. Worrying about how others might view us if we act a bit differently is usually sparked by a self-conscious energy. I believe this energy is wasteful and oftentimes makes things more stressful.

When it comes to death and dying, if someone requests you to honor them in a way that is specific to them and different from you want, it is an invitation to exercise open-mindedness. If the request is not harmful to you or anyone else, exercise that bit of courage to honor that person's perception of things.

To let go of a person is never easy. This makes it easy to want to think of the experience with death from our own point of view. It doesn't occur to us that others may possess a different vision of dying. We may walk around in fixed confidence that there is only one way to approach the grieving process or honor others we love after they've passed. I believe as long as you aren't avoiding the grief process and are at least open to honoring others' wishes, you can't help but feel more at peace and calm.

There is a high probability that most of us will experience uncertainty that makes us feel paralyzed before we die. Death is a certain ending for all of us that we will all one day face. Are you willing to meet others in their perception of death and honor, or are you fixed to let go in your way? If you were the one dying, wouldn't you wish for your family to hear and respond respectfully to your wishes? It is something worthy of contemplating.

Keep These Things in Mind

- The types of strength and stress we experience come in different forms and are personal to each individual person.
- Be okay with adding lightness to any darkness that might arise; others who take issue will get over it, and if they don't, it's their energy to live with, not yours.
- The way in which you process grief is a personal issue. It is for everyone.
- Endings can awaken peace and acceptance if you allow it.

Links to Personal Success and Peace

"*Want to be better respected and create more peace in relationships? The words, "I can't help myself" should be removed from your daily language.*"

~Amy McCann

Success Link #1: Increase Your Power to Listen

I've spoken largely about the benefits of honoring others in the beginning of this book. It is proactive to ignite good fortune and gratitude in situations.

You've hopefully become more open in your mindset when it comes to your definition of honor, strength, courage, and confidence. When you know where your behavior is coming from, you can work to be less judgmental, stressed, worried, or anxious. It's more peaceful to live a life in curious vibration of others' differences than in solid, stubborn viewpoints or ignorance.

An important link to personal success and peace is awareness of your reactions. If you are busy reacting to others, the ability to listen well ceases. Isn't it also true that it's difficult to hear others when they are busy being reactive toward us? Suddenly, we become deaf to any word they might speak.

What about these smaller ways in which we might come across as less than respectful of others in our daily interactions? I'm speaking about those little exchanges we have with people that have us spewing out our knowledge of how we think life should be rather than listening to another point of view for greater insight into things. Could our itch to voice our knowledge be plowing over others' desire to be heard?

Could poor listening be behind your spouse's frustration with you? In our efforts to help others, we sometimes offer up opinions or advice with good intent. Still, it isn't always asked for or called for. What makes us so arrogant that we can't stay focused on listening to others' concerns and thoughts. The choice to be still and listen is sometimes a very best version of yourself.

I've been guilty of not listening, so I'm not here to point fingers. I'm here to spark awareness of any potential reaction that doesn't allow for conversations to flow. Usually, I am quick to open my mouth when I haven't accessed my beginner's mind. I might be quick to respond with a know-it-all attitude not out of blatant disrespect for the other person, but out of a poor listening exchange.

I believe the four most potentially unattractive words you can speak when it comes to voicing your unwanted opinions to others are "I just can't help myself." When you can't help cutting others off in order to be heard, it's a turnoff. If you want to be better respected, consider shutting off your need to speak.

Listening Perspectives to Consider

- How would you feel about yourself if you succeeded in making a loved one's day by simply listening vs. voicing an opinion?
- Do you find it difficult or easy to imagine yourself keeping your mouth shut through a conversation?
- Do you feel it's a turnoff when others don't listen to you? If so, they might feel the same about you if you are unable to lend a listening ear.
- Do you believe a "been there, done that" attitude can come across as arrogance? Do you admire this type of interaction?
- Finally, to blow up your opinion without acknowledging or asking to hear someone's point of view first could make them feel dismissed or unimportant. To live into grace is to ignite peace, not tension into conversations. Ask yourself, "Do I need to be heard, or is it more important to try something new for the sake of grace?"

Success Link #2: Be Okay with Rejection

Have you ever worn an invisible mask in an effort to protect yourself? One way might be to try to paint a rosy picture of yourself because you're afraid of criticism or rejection. What if someone found out some ugly parts about you?

Fear is a big stress and fear of rejection if a very big one for many people. Masks come in handy to help hide that fear. The problem is, most of the time others can see right through it. They might play along but inside they might feel that being around you feels a bit disingenuous. This isn't a pleasant thought if your wish is to be authentic.

A mask to cover fear could influence others to view you as phony, boring, untrustworthy or cold (self-centered). You might reply that you don't care what others think of you and they can call you phony all they wish. This was the reply one woman gave during a group coaching session. On the heels of this she said, "If they want to judge me, that's their problem." I asked, "If that were true, that you don't care what others think, why would you wear the mask in the first place?" My intention wasn't to embarrass her. She was there to be coached. As a coach I connect to clients and students and rarely make agreements just to make people feel better. My job is to ask the tougher questions that friends aren't likely to ask. If it's uncomfortable, it means growth is occurring.

If you are wearing a mask to hide fear and protect your emotions, it is worth exploring. After all, aren't you here to persevere? If so, how can you expect to do it well if you're busy hiding?

For exploration purposes, here are three possible masks you might be wearing and questions to ponder.

Mask of Perfection

It's a social media playground of illusion out there, isn't it? It's a most convenient way to wear a virtual mask of perfection. I must say, I love my ring light! It washes out my latest age spots and mid-life acne. Still, I'm okay to keep the show going if the light goes out. I am not fearful someone might see me as less than made up or without perfectly glowing skin. Ask yourself: Do I avoid being seen as anything less than made up because I fear others might judge me? If so, a mask of perfection could be causing you anxiety. Is it worth wearing?

Mask of Safety

Do you guard yourself and your privacy like a security guard at an art museum? Is it safer to think that if you guard your heart you'll never again be hurt? By wearing a safety mask other people won't come too close. It's a sort of metaphor for illness. Come too close and we both might die. This is how many people feel after having their hearts broken. If this happens to be you, a safety mask could be preventing you from loving yourself more. To be vulnerable is to be open and raw with yourself before anyone else. If you can do this, you'll no longer have a fear of being hurt. You'll safe in the knowledge that you are loved, and you can at a last shed this safety mask!

Mask of Playtime

I love comedy. There is a dark side, however, and I'm certain you've heard about it or witnessed it. It's those times when someone is deeply depressed and manages to not only show up with a smile but make everyone around them laugh. Be careful to watch yourself. If you are being humorous to hide pain it is fooling yourself and others. This might not be the best way to get the support you need. It's up to you to decide which is more important, humor or help?

Consider this: If you believe that showing up gracefully each day also means showing up authentically, it might be worth it to start removing any masks associated with fear of rejection.

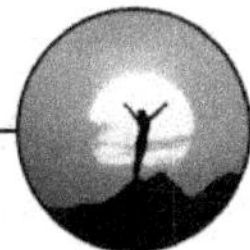

Quick Card Check-In: Fear of Rejection

Am I happy living a guarded life?

What do I fear others might find out about me?

Could I have such a need to control certain aspects of my life in order to feel safe?

Could I be fooling myself into thinking that this is the way to achieving inner peace?

Proactive Life Mastery Academy™ Amy McCann Coaching™

Success Link #3: Progress over Perfection

"Ya gotta stand being bad, if you want to be a writer."

~David Mamet

I joke that I'm a recovering perfectionist in many ways. Well, at least the bad side of perfectionism. The kind that keeps me from getting projects done. The kind that brings forth my insecurities and ego. Perfectionism is also about fear. If I fear being criticized I may never write a book. I might have to keep trying to make it perfect just to delay ever getting it out there!

I have rewritten this book many times, and that is a good thing. It means I care about what I'm doing. It means I care about the goal to make a difference in your life.

Thank goodness I've gotten over the need to control my fears through perfectionism. Ongoing attempts to improve things is an example of perseverance. I'll take process and progress over perfectionism any day.

How about you? Is today the day you'll forget the dishes and go after a bigger project you've been dreaming of completing? Are you willing to be bad at it if it means you'll learn something about yourself? The choice is yours!

Success Link #4: Connect to Your Frustration

Many years ago, I made a choice to better understand the world of home health care. Although incompetence was a factor in some cases, I guessed that stress on both ends had a lot to do with what was going on with our revolving door.

Once I got myself healthier and we had some respite care in the home, I chose to earn a nursing assistant license.

It was the third day of earning my nursing assistant license. I made a point to introduce myself and share my story from the perspective of a family receiving services. I politely expressed my discouragement in the way that professional caregivers interact with families. I asked if there was training available when it comes to understanding family caregiver stress.

As a result of opening my mouth, the instructor invited me to give a short presentation on ways I felt could help better empathize with clients and families. I said, "Imagine you woke up tomorrow to a lifetime guarantee that another person would have to help you with your most intimate needs. How does it make you feel?"

Then, answers slowly trickled in. I remember the words "I'm a better caregiver than I am a patient, that I know." Another woman chimed, "I don't want to think about it." The discussion helped lead us all back to a reconnection to what it feels like to put yourself in another's shoes.

I managed to connect with one student after class. She claimed she couldn't understand why Mr. J, who was assigned to her at her previous job, was so crotchety. This had bothered her for some time. She hadn't considered his possible need to feel in control or that he might be stressed. She hadn't wanted to imagine herself in his position. She simply wanted to care for him. She said, "I just couldn't understand why he couldn't see that I was there to help him."

This woman wasn't aware that her client might see her not as a caring professional, but as a stranger invading his space. She said she had been really upset that he didn't appreciate her attempts to make him feel comfortable. Now, she said she felt like she could take better care of any next client that wasn't so pleasant. This small talk the teacher invited me to share seemed to help alleviate some of her discouragement and stress when she thought about the client. She admitted that she wouldn't like it if she needed someone to take care of her. She said, "I would be grateful for the help, but I would also need time adjusting. Isn't this true of us all?

It took new action to speak up in class to gain insight into issues that were bothering me. I had to get out there and do some work. To my surprise, I helped someone in the process. You can do the same in any situation you're in. Seek to find opportunities to help you understand more. Insights are valuable educational nuggets and do work to release tension caused by frustration. They can also work to help someone else.

Additional Personal Success Habits

Keep Learning

While earning my Bachelor of Science in Psychology, I chose to do my final report on the topic of stress among direct support workers. Statistics still reflect 60-80% turnover rates among direct support workers in home health organizations in the first year of employment. Why such a high turnover rate? It isn't the low pay rate, as you might guess. It is high emotional stress and burnout.

Researchers repeatedly report a lack of, and recommendation for, stress management programs among these agencies as a way to increase job retention and fill the gap home care services.

A better understanding of caregiver stress helped me reflect upon what happened in those days of rotating caregivers. My interest in addressing my relationship with disappointment has carried to today. A choice to engage with continued learning is how I am better able to help you in the face of overwhelming circumstances. What will you choose to learn today and how might it help someone?

Shed the Need to Control Everything

When was the last time you felt you needed to control things? Does it drive you crazy when others don't do things the way you do them? My husband Sean is the family chef. Each time he cooks, I question whether the Swedish chef charier from *The Muppets* has stopped by for a visit. How exactly do you get a pile of peas to fly to the top of a kitchen cabinet?

I've learned to live in better grace of what others do—especially if it's done as a loving gesture. So what if I slipped on another potato peel? Big deal. I managed to break both my feet by just walking down the stairs, so who am I to say a potato peel might be a hazard?

It used to drive me crazy when the pepper was positioned to my right and the salt to my left. Talk about control issues. Today, I might still catch myself to position things in a way that helps me feel balanced. It's a weird thing, but at least it isn't harming anyone! Still, it speaks something about an old internal habit to want to feel in control of certain things in order to feel better somehow.

If your hours are spent trying to control everything, it can set you up to crash when bigger things show up. The good news is we can influence our own way out of control and into more peaceful flow to simply agree to let things go. This is one way to embrace others more openly. It is a mutual benefit to learn to let things go because there is more peace and less stress. In many cases, it is a sign of respect to step back and just observe, appreciate, and allow others to flow to the speed of their own vibration and way of doing things.

Additional Success Habits Considerations

Learning is a never-ending process that doesn't end until we are dead. What might you choose to do today that feeds a learning or creative desire?

The feeling that you need to control others might come out of a need to feel in control of yourself. What is one thing you might let go of this week that would improve a relationship in your life?

Moving forward, is it worth it to shut down others just to satisfy your annoyance with the way they do things? If someone's way of doing things is distasteful to you, you might consider how your opinion might be negatively charging the relationship.

Proactive Life Mastery Academy™ Amy McCann Coaching™

PERSEVERANCE WORKSHEET

As a success in perseverance exercise, here are some questions I asked myself and what you can ask yourself to move you out of feeling stuck in frustration:

Am I sick and tired of feeling so anxious? If so, is it worth it to me to challenge myself to let go of some ideas, fears, or judgements I might have today?

____

____

____

Do I believe I can speak to people in a way that is influencing rather than controlling? If so, how? If not, why?

____

____

____

Would I describe myself as a leader or a controlling micromanager in training to learn to lead?

____

____

____

____

Habit #3: Visual Trigger to Ignite Strong Habits

Light Up Monthly Vision to Succeed

Adapted from Proactive Life Mastery Academy™ Online Training in Perseverance

Third-Level Perseverance-Habit #3: Success

Pyramid of Perseverance:
AMC Proactive Levels to Success™

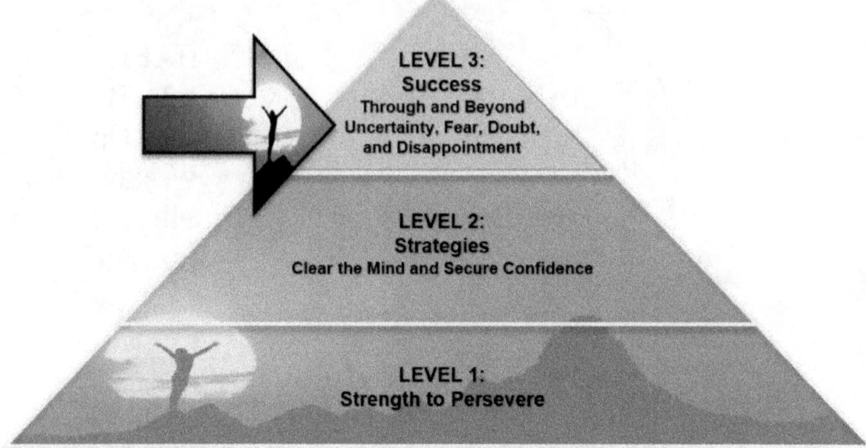

Adapted from Proactive Life Matters Academy™ Online Training in Perseverance
Personal Commitments Guide to Success Worksheet
Designed by, Amy McCann Coaching™

CHAPTER 12
FUTURE NEW BEGINNINGS

Visions Realized: A Story of Success through Obstacles

I had clearly imagined this moment thousands of times. "Oh, my God! Oh, my God! Oh, my God!" My husband spoke for both of us as we witnessed this miracle hovering above our heads. Our first baby girl was outstretched in the safety of the doctor's hands. It was just seconds after she popped into world for the first time. I felt a mix of relief and frozen anticipation as we awaited our second miracle, another baby girl, to make her entrance. One minute later, we heard her tiny cries echo off the walls.

It was nine years since the day we chose to start a new beginning together as a couple. We were now at the very beginning of the uncertainties of parenthood, and I felt more prepared than ever. My commitment to self-care had paid off and a new vision was realized.

I share this section to help you see that anything is possible when you are strong enough to face new obstacles along the way. Making a choice to do what is different from other people always comes with a price. People will judge you. People will abandon you. People will disappoint you over and over again. Some people will be scared of your strength and voice criticism whenever possible. People will doubt your capabilities. Now that you've learned to persevere these people will simply remind you to keep learning. You'll no longer be bothered to the point of emotional paralysis.

It took three rounds of failed In-Vitro Fertilization attempts to finally achieve success in pregnancy. It was a process met with much criticism. In one circumstance a woman said, "Why on God's green earth would you try to have a baby when you can adopt?" It was a bit curious to hear considering she chose to give birth to three biological children. Did she feel a disabled person can't raise a child? Did she feel her three children tipped the world's population over the edge? Could it be she thought we would not succeed in producing babies? The possibilities are endless! The important thing is, I made no final assumptions as to why she felt this way. Frankly, I didn't wish to engage with the conversation, so I politely excused myself.

Becoming a strong mother took development in all the areas I share with you in this book. Personal growth was (and is) an uphill battle at times. Now, instead of staring up at a flickering hospital light, I was staring into the eyes of two baby humans. This was the difference between a stressful life and a calmer inner confidence and courage to succeed. Bringing my babies to my chest, I sunk into the depth of this new ability to love.

Struggles Have Advantages

I want to encourage you to explore the advantages of going through a struggle. It will help you appreciate the fact that you stayed committed to something difficult. I no longer feel confused about my strengths. I feel gratitude for others who have shown me ways to be a stronger person. You can, too!

Here's my secret advantage with struggle. As a caregiver for a decade I had a secret advantage over other parents my age who were shocked by the amount of work that goes into attending to a new baby. If you think about it, I was in good practice of sleep deprivation from my earlier days adjusting to our situation. I already knew what it was like to wake up three times a night and had done it for years. It was much easier to nurse two six-pound babies than reposition a full-grown adult. I knew what it was like to manually and gruelingly strap down a 300 lb. wheelchair to the floor of our vehicle. This made trapping babies into car seats a cinch. Nursing twins was a challenge, but I persevered successfully for one year. I could do this because I was now healthy and strong in mind, body and spirit.

If you have endured struggle and even if you persevered in survival mode, it's still important to pull some positives out of the situation. As you can see, struggle has its advantages.

Beginner's Confidence to Ignite Personal Success

It took a focus in three things to successfully transition into parenthood against all odds and in light of the challenges as a caregiver:

- A beginner's mindset to overcome judgments from others
- A willingness to let old goals go and embrace uncertainty in new ways
- A new vision for personal success

Beginner's Mindset Ignites Motion

My husband was long past the days when he struggled to keep rice on his fork. He had surpassed what the doctors expected, including becoming a biological father to twin girls. Most of the home health nightmares were long over. Now, we were hiring our own part-time private attendants twice a week as new residents of New Hampshire.

I was still working my business as a direct marketing consultant training a team of twenty-five leaders. I had a light, fun, and flexible job that made it possible to work around the challenges of parenting, caregiving, and time with my husband. Still, it wasn't a flexible job that made my life less stressful.

It was a beginner's mindset that allowed me to open the door to a new relationship with disappointment. It was a beginner's mindset that asked, "How can I interact more effectively with the caregivers I am training?" I had to let go of my tightness to privacy. I had to be open and welcoming of people who were there to help rather than living in tight-chested expectation that they might disappoint.

I had finally moved past pushing toward goals that had long expired. I worked to grieve through some things that I hadn't faced in the six years that passed. A beginner's mindset got me unstuck from a belief that I had to stick to a life plan that I had outgrown. I got off the acting career track, which was no longer as meaningful to me in my overall expansion as a person. I got excited to create and expand myself in ways that included all I had learned about courage to take risks and ability to keep the show going even if I had a risk of falling. None of this was done perfectly. This was about personal progress. I would fall many times over and was ready to prevent unnecessary bruising. This is what I hope to have done for you by providing you these exercises in this book.

Perseverance Pays off in Good Fortune

"Good things come to those who persevere."

~Amy McCann

Good fortune follows when you are willing to make changes. The home health aides we hired fourteen years ago are still with us. Our daughters have been fortunate to have grown up with them since birth and to have known them each fondly. When you work with your stress and fears more intentionally, you invite calm in others. The staying power of a caregiver isn't guaranteed. Still, if you work to communicate better and understand more of what you and other people are struggling with, good things happen.

More good fortune bloomed as fellow professional peers made swimming in the ocean an accessible option for my husband. I had earned a free cruise for two in my leadership role with a direct sales company. It was a time to celebrate a few successes and ignite more gratitude.

It was a most precarious and vulnerable adventure to watch my husband take a soak in the ocean. It ended in a successful float among the warm waves of the Caribbean water. Salty tears met with the salty ocean as I witnessed my husband triumph over one more obstacle. With a few sets of willing helping hands and the courage to trust, anything is possible.

Shortly following this cruise, I received a call from a company reporter. We were asked if we would be interested in being interviewed and featured in a family first segment as a company marketing story. By coincidence, I was volunteering and chairing the committee of our local Relay for Life on behalf of the American Cancer Society the weekend of filming. This made it possible to video-capture other members of my family, including my brother, who were participating in the fundraiser for the fight against cancer.

A professional videographer was sent to our home after a few laps around the relay field. I sat perched on a tall kitchen chair. I spoke the first words of my story as the light on his camera turned green. The question, "How did you do it?" was again at the forefront of what others were interested in learning about my lifestyle. "How is it that you manage things, running a successful business, dealing with the obstacles of disability, and raising three-year-old twins? What can you tell others in the industry about balancing it all?"

After the first take of sharing the "why" behind how I was doing things, the videographer wiped tears from his eyes. I was surprised to see that what I had shared moved him. I came to realize that when you value your efforts, struggles, and strengths, you serve to move some people in ways that might surprise you. More meaningful connections are made when do the work to participate in life. When you've worked through some stress, disappointment, and fears, you have a power to open a door to people's spirits and emotions.

I was no longer dismissive or quiet about my life. I was confident in expressing my weaknesses and strengths. This small opportunity to speak knocked, and I opened the door. It turns out my story might matter a little further beyond our four walls. I gained more clarity in what it was I had accomplished. This tiny video worked to inspire so many people that I could no longer ignore answering the question, "How do you do it?"

I had figured out the deeper meaning behind what people were really asking: "How can I have more courage in the face of uncertainty? How can I be more confident to step into tough situations? How is it that you're standing, and I feel like I'm falling apart?"

A New Vision of Personal Success Blooms

This videographer created a beautifully moving snapshot of our family. Like a pair of singing Marias from *The Sound of Music,* our three-year-old twins could be seen spinning around in a large open field. At one point, the video panned to my brother, a childhood burn survivor, walking in support alongside cancer survivors. Once again, his integrity to show up and participate made me proud to be his sister.

This time, the lump in my throat that formed wasn't from fear or uncertainty. I was feeling the emotion from a crowd of thousands in response to what the videographer had created. To me, watching our little family on the big screen was not a marketing snippet of what's possible in your life and business. It was a larger vision of my personal journey toward confidence to speak up and answer the question, "How do you do it?" It was a small bit of evidence that I had persevered past a stressful relationship with self-doubt through uncertainty. From out of the ashes of personal despair at times, personal success bloomed as a result of my efforts. Now, it seemed, that good fortune was being passed on as a gift to others.

Quick Check-In: Vision and Goals

Process: This is a tool you can access every six months or once a year to check in with your life vision and goals.

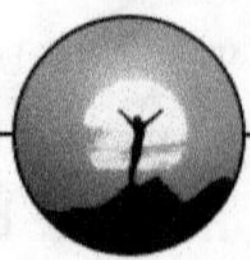

Quick Card Six Month or Yearly Check-In: Vision and Goals

CLARITY

Does my vision for the future still apply to my life circumstance?

CONNECTION

When I think of my goals, are they as meaningful to me as they once were?

CONSIDERATION

If I let go of these goals to create a new vision, who might it effect?

COMMUNICATION

When can I schedule a time to discuss my idea with this person?

ACTION

What action steps can I incorporate into my calendar that will help bring me closer to letting go of what is holding me back?

Proactive Life Mastery Academy™ Amy McCann Coaching™

CHAPTER 13
VISION TO IGNITE ABUNDANT LIVING

Level 3: Success

Peace and Harmony This Way

"Your vision will become clear only when you look into your heart. Who looks outside dreams. Who looks inside awakens."

~Carl Jung

You're getting closer to feeling more personally peaceful and successful in the face of uncertainty.

If you've been following along with the exercises, you should:

- Feel more self-inspired and empowered to face uncertainty, fear, doubt, and disappointment.
- Feel more confident in your commitment to self to take better care of your overall health.
- Understand that a proactive life is what will make the difference in your effectiveness; this will lower your stress and get you thinking more clearly.

- Understand the difference between healthy and unhealthy perseverance.

As we move forward, you will reach your final level of perseverance and personal success. You won't simply feel successful, you will have participated in the success-driven proactive actions I've laid out in this book. I will take you on a journey through your pyramid shortly to show you how your day might play out when you implement these actions.

How to Have A More Abundant Life When You Think You Have So Little Time

In different ways, many people ask, "How can I have the things I want in life when there is so much responsibility?" What people really want to know is, "How will I ever have time for me?"

Personal success is a journey that includes persevering beyond mindset constraints. If you keep telling yourself there just isn't time, you create mental constraints. You begin to imagine yourself toiling away with only a yearly vacation in sight to relieve you. All of us have felt there isn't enough time for ourselves, our hobbies, or anything that brings life to our spirits. It's our job to break free of those thoughts. It's our freedom to follow what our hearts say.

Hopefully I've helped inspire you to let go of the idea that it takes a lot of time to take care of yourself. Abundance is in the result of taking better care of yourself. If you're stretched and ready to snap, how on earth could you ever expect to create more for yourself within the twenty-four hours you are given in a day? It isn't time, but energy, that you need more of. It's everything we've been talking about in this book.

As a reminder, I will once again bullet-point below what you've journeyed through in this book. It doesn't take a lot of time to create higher levels of abundance in energy. Without attention to your energy and health, it doesn't matter how much time you have in a day. You'll be too exhausted to enjoy yourself!

You have gained much by way of committing to this entire process to Persevere to Succeed. You have a new advantage after doing (and continuing to do) the following:

- A courageous commitment to your self-care
- A visual tool reminder to trigger daily, weekly, and monthly habits that set you up for success
- The Whole Health Check-In for your emotional, physical, daily, and spiritual awareness and progress
- The Pyramid of Perseverance Model
- The Three-Level Proactive Approach to Succeed
- The Proactive Lifestyle Model to increase your awareness

There is little connection sometimes to what is most meaningful to us individually and apart from our external responsibilities. It's difficult to see this connection when so much disappointment, stress, doubt, and fear gets in the way. You must learn to ignite a clear-thinking ability to why you're not moving in the direction you'd like in life.

If you've been paying attention to what you're reading, I work to help connect you to your awareness about your stress response in relation to uncertainty. If you're uncertain how to build an abundant life, you will remain ambiguous. Set to work on the things I've been sharing, and you'll move beyond ambiguity.

You might say your family is the most meaningful thing. If that's true, do you only work to put food on the table, or do you also work to create beauty within your family? You might say, "Amy, you don't understand. I have a job that demands my attention. I'm realistic. I have to meet my responsibilities as a single parent. I'm stretched thin as it is. What is this beauty of which you speak?"

Beauty by my definition is a persevering lifestyle that considers all areas as worthy of attention. The ugly devils of uncertainty, fear, doubt, and disappointment are always on deck to scare you from having it all. Believe me, you can have it all without all the stress. You can learn to only focus on the things that contribute to what's most meaningful to you.

Abundant living in my eyes is an ability to create and bring to life a vision you have of all that is meaningful to you. This means actively creating a vision and then doing the work to ignite the fruits of your labor.

Gifts of Wisdom to Ignite Abundant Success

"Abundant living is an ability to create and bring to life a vision of what is most beautiful or meaningful to you."

~Amy McCann

Crouched between two rows of pumpkins, I couldn't decide which one to choose for the front steps of our new home. By now, my husband and I had left the city life behind and returned to my roots in New Hampshire.

My stepfather Bill, to whom I refer as the father who raised me, grew over a hundred pumpkins. It was time for his biological and stepchildren and many grandchildren on both sides to pick their favorite to either carve or decorate with. Across the yard lived a large family of sunflowers and sweet or tart apples on which to munch if you got hungry.

What makes Bill's presence in the world more meaningful are the fields of vegetable and flower gardens that he so lovingly planted and tends to. He's built these gardens for over thirty years, and they are simply abundant in fragrance and flavor. Gardens are always the perfect example of the hard patience someone puts in to make them flourish.

I share this next reflection of Bill and my parents to challenge you to think differently when it comes to time, patience, and the ability to live an abundantly full life. It may spark you to reignite a hobby you've given up that brings fulfillment. You might relieve yourself of the idea that there just isn't time to do things you want to do.

In addition to his role as a dedicated business owner and factory worker, my stepfather invested much patience and energy into bringing the property to life. The land that was once peppered in ashy mounds of dirt is now a storybook picture of green grass, hand-built rock walls, and a wide assortment of food and flowers. To the left is a very old pine tree whose branch still holds a tire swing from when I was little.

Imagine standing on a rock wall. It is surrounded by a variety of multi-colored rose bushes, peonies, irises, daffodils, and many other colorful flowers. Across the way is a hand-built pond stocked with fish. Each spring, my mother scoops a couple out with a net to keep in the house as a fish tank pet. To the left of the pond is a large pumpkin patch and many rows of raspberry bushes. To the right, depending on the time of year, there is a wealth of zucchini, cucumber, asparagus, carrots, tomatoes, blueberries, lettuce, and corn.

On the surrounding property, there are hundreds more flowers. Lilac tress and a variety of apple trees, cherry trees, and pear trees are there to pick from. It is an abundant oasis that my mother designed, and my stepfather nourishes. Out of the berries and tomatoes, my mother makes several different kinds of jellies and jams and cans many jars of tomatoes for sauce. Bill is a master berry pie maker. Their homemade pies and jellies are my most favorite Christmas gifts.

Success Ingredient: Integrity

"A person of integrity is what we should all seek to observe. I learned from my stepfather that integrity is a masterpiece of personal and business success."

~Amy McCann

I was seated at the kitchen table finishing the final touches on the hand-drawn wolf spider for a school project. My mother walked in the door with her date, Bill. I was just shy of thirteen and had gotten to know my mother as a single parent for the last two years.

The day my mother announced her choice to divorce my biological father was a day my shoulders relaxed. It wasn't that I didn't love my father. I simply felt relieved that I could finally step out of what I felt was a continuous and scary ghost story. Poof, he was home, poof, he was gone. Poof, he might show, poof, he might not.

My mother's face had changed. Her eyes appeared brighter and less puffy than usual. She reached across the table to tell me the news of the impending divorce. I squeezed her hand tightly. I then leaped to wrap my arms around her and express how happy I felt that things were changing.

On my mother's date night with Bill, he casually strolled over to my wolf spider project. It wouldn't take long to feel completely at ease and peace with his kind-natured being. Bill is a special kind of person I don't often meet. His non-complaining work ethic and integrity ignite immediate confidence that the world is indeed a kinder place than we might feel it is.

The winter of my fifteenth birthday, Bill became a husband to my mother and my cherished stepfather. There were no more disappearing acts of which to be fearful. My stepfather proved to be a model of trust and stability.

Bill's work ethic is to be admired, in my opinion. He operated his long-time successful trash removal business in the early mornings. He then went to work in the local electric wire mill in the next town over. He worked both morning and night shifts before and after his day shift at the factory to complete his trash removal route. After all this, he still made time and had the patience to see me through algebra.

How to Build Abundant Success (without All the Stress)

My parents continue to create a life of overflowing abundance that keeps on giving. This, to me, is personal success at its finest.

The key in opening the door to success is to connect yourself often back to your first-level proactive building block: secure a purpose to ignite good fortune and gratitude. My stepfather is the master at exercising gratitude.

Here are my stepfather's top three gifts of wisdom, perceived and translated from my point of view. I now gift them to you:

Gift #1: Faith Perspective: Growing Wisdom from my Stepfather

It may not be a lack of time that's holding you back from creating inner peace and abundance. It could be that you're spending too much time thinking about the wrong things.

If you want to grow a garden, it isn't extra time you need, it is energy and patience. It also takes faith that the earth's ground will work to support your efforts to sow a seed.

Gift #2: Patience Perspective Growing Wisdom from my Stepfather

You need the intelligent insight that even with faith, the earth's efforts may fail you. A plant may not survive. A deer may eventually come dig up and destroy your hours of work. This is where you discover that peace lives in the patience to keep sowing. You need patience even in the face of disappointment or doubt.

Gift #3: Vision Perspective Growing Wisdom from my Stepfather

You don't actually have to love or have passion for your job to live a happy life.

If you have a meaningful vision of what you'd like to build, and the job you're not so crazy about is succeeding in getting you there, then it is best to appreciate, not hate your job. This is mindset abundance.

Other Lessons Learned from my Parents

- You can get a lot done and still experience peace.
- Things do not have to be harried, miserable, or stressful in order to have a successful life.
- It is possible to carry a successful business and a full-time job, plan a meaningful and relaxing family vacation, spend quality time with loved ones, and still look forward to engaging with a hobby. You just need to put your heart and energy in the right place.

Life is Rarely as Difficult as We Make It

To create a greater life of abundance, you must learn to shift your mindset and focus on what's most meaningful to you. When you can do that, the pieces simply fall into place like the masterful piece worker you are!

HABIT #3: A MONTHLY VISIONARY WORKSHEET

Ignite: On the first of each month, consider setting a personal vision for yourself for the next four weeks using this guide. Track your progress using a chart similar to the one below.

Celebrate: At the end of the year, you will have accomplished twelve total visionary practices.

My vision for this month is:

____

____

Example: financially motivated, spiritually motivated, relationship motivated, educationally motivated.

The action I will take to fulfill my vision will be to:

____

____

Example: set aside ten dollars a day to purchase the event VIP package by the end of the month to fulfill my educational motivation to succeed.

Sample Visionary Track Sheet

MONTH #1 Clear-Minded Outlook	Beginning of Week Action Step Planned	End of Week Action Accountability	End of Month Visionary Success
WEEK ONE	***example: set aside ten dollars a day***	✔	✔
WEEK TWO			
WEEK THREE			
WEEK FOUR			

Proactive Life Mastery Academy™ Amy McCann Coaching™

CHAPTER 14
HARMONY/PEACE/SUCCESS

A Long Season Ends, New Success Ignites

"Now this is not the end. It is not even the beginning of the end. But it is, perhaps, the end of the beginning."

~Winston Churchill

A thumbtack held its position in the wall after it had been retired of its purpose. The echo of the house key dropping to the table rippled through my spine. The walls in front of me were bare, except for the squares that were once covered by photos of times past.

With each breath, my nose was met with familiar scent of jasmine that lingered from a nearby oil essentials infuser. The tires of my husband's power wheelchair squeaked across the recently mopped hardwood floors. Two years before, we spent days picking out flooring when the new house addition was built. His expression stirred something in me I hadn't felt in a while—a feeling of deep loss along with a conviction that this was another new beginning for us to which I was committed.

The last time I felt this way was when my husband (then, my boyfriend), was lying in a stark hospital room in Canada. The most specialized spinal cord doctors in the world tended to a motionless body as a result of his permanent paralysis. I remembered that day so long ago like it was yesterday. We'd come so far since I held his face and spoke those four words: "This is a new beginning."

It was a mutual decision to divorce and the ending of a very long season of overcoming hardship and being met with many blessings. On this day, as we prepared to part ways as married partners, our eyes locked. I believe there was an unspoken mutual relief and sadness exchanged in the decision we had made. Our twin daughters, now five years old, had been prepared for the separation weeks before.

It wasn't all rosy, as the divorce process is stressful. I had to renew my relationship with the Fiery Four.

Post-Divorce Wisdom

People now ask how I do it in relation to how well I get along with my ex-husband. For a while, I believed I had nothing to share in the way of post-divorce success or the co-parenting relationship. After all, isn't divorce personal? How could I inspire people to get along with their ex? I just left at the thought that I was one of the lucky few people who has a friendly ex.

Then, I realized I had been missing out on an opportunity to share some valuable secrets behind happiness after divorce. First, I had to remind myself that it is not simply that my ex is friendly. I had worked really consistently on improving myself post-divorce. I hit obstacles and went backwards a few times, but I found my way back by doing what I've taught you in this book.

If you are going through a divorce, what I can say to you is this:

- Any one of the Fiery Four Devils might threaten to burn you out or burn you down. Be confident that you know how to handle them!
- You are an individual. Your ex has nothing to do with your measure of progress as a human

being. It is never too early to change your mindset from believing things are difficult to believing it is a challenge and opportunity to empower yourself. Don't wait for a long round of therapy sessions before you tend to your gratitude and courage.

- Remember to grieve, not wallow. The difference between these looks like this:

  Healthy Grief: I feel the loss deeply. I know this means it's because I loved deeply. I'm not afraid of these feelings even if they hurt badly because they can teach me something.

  Wallowing/Self-Pity: I read somewhere to give yourself permission to wallow during brief timed sessions. I believe in this. It allows for negative thoughts and feeling to be expelled in a structured amount of time. I find this time to be cathartic. Still, if you wallow unchecked, it can linger and hold you back. It might look like this: Why did this happen to me? Why did she leave me? Why do I have to be the one to role model for the kids? Why did I have to marry such a jerk?

Your ex may, in fact, be the devil, and now you know how to handle the devils in your life!

When a relationship ends, there is a history that exists between two people. You could try to bury that history, but like it or not, it's a part of you. I believe that history should be cherished to the extent that you've loved and learned some lessons about yourself in relation to another person. It may not be helpful to wonder if this person you spent time with was truly invested in you. It might only serve to ignite uncertainty paralysis.

I believe that if you entered into relationships with good intentions to love fully, you can exit with all the same intention of bidding a person farewell should he or she exercise the free will to leave. At the same time, allow the grieving process and begin to recognize where you need to grow.

I believe what makes my transition into co-parenting successful isn't about the fact that my ex-husband and I don't hate each other. Still, this is what most people focus on and what they wish to achieve "for the sake of the children." They ask, "Amy, how can I get my ex to answer my calls, so we can show the kids we get along? Doesn't she know how stupid she's being? Why can't she see her behavior is hurting the children? How can I get him to respect me? He says horrible things to the kids about me, and it's completely unacceptable! Help me figure out how I can get him to stop!" If you can remember that it's not at all about what you could do to stop, control, or persuade your ex to change, you can focus on how you can control your reactions. Isn't this a most loving way to influence your children?

One more thing: It is true that some exes will go to great lengths to destroy your reputation or drag the kids through the mud. Some people find their satisfaction in hurting you for some internal reason of their own. Yes, these types of reactions can cause real damage to families. Still, we are here to concentrate your efforts in perseverance from a self-inspired, clear lens to handle your reactions to these things more calmly, intelligently, and courageously.

Third-Level Success through Major Transition

What happens when you reach your point of success? In our case, we are moving toward a third level of success that represents a higher level of peace through uncertainty. This peace comes from the efforts to be proactive throughout your day, week, month, and year. It is a point at which you can celebrate your choice to engage with new methods of building strength for yourself. The extended advantage and benefit in all of this is that your relationships will be stronger as well.

You've stuck with this process, and that means you're committed to persevering. These efforts you've engaged with shouldn't be taken lightly. Many people wish for their circumstances to be better. This may have been you prior to picking up this book. Now, you know there are ways to act to change your circumstances that don't have to be stressful.

A Walk Through Your Pyramid

Let's take a moment to celebrate you. Let's take you through your pyramid to imagine how your day, week, month, and year might play out as you engage with the persevering habits you've explored. Imagine each level of the pyramid represents a segment of time. The first level represents your day, the second level represents your month, and the third level the year.

Let's say it's the first Sunday of the month. This is the day you've chosen to incorporate a monthly intelligent plan and path of courage. To do this is to incorporate the tools you've explored in this book. No worries about which tools you'll use. You won't have to flip through these chapters searching for them, either. You can request an easy-to-follow Proactive Planning Guide that incorporates all that you've explored by emailing my team: amy@3dstresssolutionscoach.com.

Making a habit to commit to a daily, weekly, and monthly plan will create dramatic and lasting change your life. Developing new habits doesn't have to be a boring process! Here's how I've made a difference in my financial life, for example. My husband Sean and I meet each and every Saturday morning for a scheduled money meeting. We actually started doing this when we were engaged to be married as a proactive effort to understand each other's financial stresses and goals better. Even when we are on vacation, we stick to this money meeting. We may allow flexibility in the time we meet, but we are committed to sticking to our plan. Over coffee, we follow a process from the book *For Richer, Not Poorer: The Money Book for Couples* by Ruth Hayden. This simple habit of meeting each week removes financial stress. There is no need to argue because we know there is a scheduled time to discuss any issues that follow a structure.

This is what I hope to provide you with—a structure and plan to follow that creates dramatic progress and lowers stress. You are already a success for choosing to go this far in the book. Are you ready to ignite success and persevere with energy?

Let’s take our imaginary walk through your pyramid and bring these tools to life!

First-Level Pyramid of Perseverance: Gratitude and Grace

It is morning. You are on the first level of your pyramid. You arise to ignite gratitude and grace for the day. Instead of generating worry about what might happen later, you choose to put focus and attention on your closest relationships. In the shower, you go through the three-step process to imagine how you might show up for someone you care about today. 1.) Pick someone to *appreciate.* 2.) *Contemplate* what action step you might take generates gratitude. 3.) If possible, immediately *initiate* this action step prior to going to work. Take five minutes to journal in the morning or before bed. You may want to access the Life-Lasting Gifts Worksheet to connect to any wisdom you might have gained that could help you move forward. As a gift to yourself, fill in the Whole Health Worksheet.

Second-Level Pyramid of Perseverance: Intelligent Thinking and Planning/Courage

It is the first Sunday of the month. This is your time to create a monthly goal. To do this, you will fill in the Monthly Visionary Worksheet. To generate courage this month, you decide to use the Balanced Self-Care Guide to build emotional, mindset, and persevering strength. To save time, you might wish to use the Quick Card Weekly Check-In for Courage. Based on the Proactive Planning Guide at the end of this book, you can choose a to interact with any or all of tools that suit your life at the moment. Complete this time with yourself by celebrating or congratulating yourself in some way for sticking to your commitment.

Third-Level Pyramid of Perseverance: Vision and Strength

Why not celebrate your success in moving through your year with more perseverance on your birthday? This is a great day to remember to check in to your emotional, physical, spiritual, and mental health. It's your birthday, so give yourself the gift of extra attention to grace, courage, wisdom, and strength.

When it comes to reaching a point of success in anything, it's important to remember that there will still be obstacles. I consider my transition out of my first marriage and my co-parenting relationship with my ex a success. There isn't one thing I've chosen to explore or commit to in life I consider a failure. This is a choice in mindset. Another person may see my divorce as a failure in keeping a marriage together. This opinion is none of my business.

It can help to remember that this entire journey on which I've taken you is about process. There is no ending to growth or obstacles, so doesn't it make sense that there is no end to success?

What you've engaged with in this book is a lifestyle of persevering habits. These are the things that serve to help you through uncertainty and also when you've hit the level of success you've been aiming at.

A success point is not an end. It is a beginning of another round of tests, turns, obstacles, and new ways to challenge yourself. This is not what most of us want to hear. We wish for ease and a worry-free existence. Peace is at the top of our success model. This doesn't mean you won't have days where peace is challenged. People won't always admire you for your calmer way of reacting to things. Some people are used to dealing with life in dramatic ways and aren't always comfortable when others are calmer in the face of hardship.

The road to successfully getting through uncertainty begins today.

Obstacle Awareness

Perseverance is about everything we've talked about in the book. It focuses on these obstacles at hand that could be holding you back:

- Any negative stress response and reactions in the face of uncertainty
- Any unrealized weaknesses as a result of self-doubt or lack in self-care
- Any fears associated with a lack of confidence
- Any negative reactions to disappointment

Now that you've worked through how to approach these obstacles, your next step in deeper awareness is to recognize the obstacles you might be creating for yourself. I see one mistake of which most people aren't aware when it comes to persevering through unforeseen or chosen transitions. I call it *obstacle obsession.* This often stops people from experiencing a higher level of personal success.

Think about it: When was the last time you were obsessed with someone else's success? Did this become an obstacle to your happiness throughout the day? Did you obsess over a person's luck or talent so much that you've now created a paralyzing obstacle in jealousy? Do you become obsessed with the thought that you could never do what they are doing? These are examples of obstacle obsessions, and all are completely controlled by you.

Following major transitions, there are many ways we create new obstacles for ourselves. We push as if our lives depend on it. In reality, we are very good at creating hardships that don't have to exist in the first place. This is worse than any financial worries you may have played out in your head. When it comes to money, you will eventually figure out how to make things work when you come from a beginner's mindset and not from a place of lack. The obstacles of which I speak that I believe are worse than financial ones are the ones over which you have no control and work hard to fix.

One uncontrollable obstacle I see is to adopt a survival-style approach in dealing with an ex's behavior following a breakup or divorce. Worry becomes the obstacle as you might work hard to change an ex's behavior in front of the kids, for example. You worry you might collapse if this person doesn't change. When you choose to turn your back on this worry to focus on your reactions, you build strength. You will persevere through upsets without the burden of trying to change things or burning down emotionally in the process.

Consequences of Belief Obstacles

If you come to believe you're too old to learn you are effectively creating your own self-limiting obstacle. The greater consequence might be that you feel less alive. If you want to achieve personal success more often, you must be willing to relieve yourself of some belief obstacles. When you do you are guaranteed to come alive.

Extinguish Burning Beliefs: Ignite Empowering Behaviors

What makes my divorce successful is that I am focused on being the best individual I can be. I believe this is what my ex-husband strives for as well. There is no goal of trying to change or control my ex-husband. His behavior is his to own. My behavior is mine to own. I realize the good fortune that I married a person who is on that same level to put energy into internal self-care. This models a healthy communication style for our girls. Still, it is what we do as individuals that matters most in the long run. My empowering belief is that I am capable of generating peace within myself, even if my ex turned into a devil tomorrow.

My ex-husband and I communicate regularly and have had many lunches together (including with my new husband) with our kids. This makes many people raise their eyebrows. They ask, "How could you possibly have lunch with your ex?" One woman summed up her discomfort rather bluntly: "Amy, it's just so weird." What if we see things as weird because of a belief that there is only one way to view divorce?

Divorce is like death — a collection of lived moments has come to an end. Two differences lie in the grieving process, in my opinion. In death, we usually do well to include honoring moments when that life existed in vibration with others. In the case of divorce, there is an epidemic disrespect for a life still living (the ex) as we grieve what once was with that person.

Does this mean we should pay our honoring respects to the ex that dumped us? What I believe is this: Unless you're prepared to spit on your ex's grave in front of your children, you shouldn't be willing to spit in his or her face while above ground either. To do so might be to disrespect our loving natures. Sometimes a loving nature simply means to be still, observe, and focus on how our reactions could affect others. Choose to extinguish burning beliefs to get back at someone and ignite empowering behaviors.

Benefits of Removing Self-Imposed Obstacles

- Banishing an obsession to be focused on things over which you have no control.
- Becoming your greatest self-advocate.
- Standing tall in self-respect, firm in self-care, and flexible in the face of uncertainty.

These, to me, are clear of example of mature personal success.

All of the exercises in this book bring you right back to your awareness of your strengths and how you might use them to build energy. No other person has the power to imprison your thoughts. They are yours to own and yours to stop you or propel you forward. Your job and your relationships are not prison sentences or end-of-the-road growth for you. Each serves its purpose to help you develop a better relationship with the Fiery Four. You can either allow them to burn you down or to ignite successful behavior.

One More Reason to Return to Beginner's Mindset

Both of our daughters transitioned so well through divorce, it took them a long time to understand why other children cried over parents separating. The children's divorce books that I read to them seemed to confuse them. "Mommy, why is the baby bear crying because daddy's going back to his house? Doesn't he know daddy's coming back tomorrow to mommy's house?"

A connection back to a beginner's mind helped me remember to teach my daughters that many possibilities exist in the ways in which people experience situations. It was my job to help them see that others might experience divorce differently. It is my job to help uncover the most common things people suffer when feelings of loss set in. Once they understood, they gained empathy. Now their ears were available to gently hear the cries of any classmates whose parents were separated or divorced.

Divorce became an opportunity for our family to experience a whole other level of trust and closeness. Many seasons have turned over, and now we were in the next season of co-parenting. As a couple, we had toiled, managed, gone on missions, advocated, and came out better for it in our individual ways. From the start, I used a beginner's mindset. It evolved from optimistic thinking to more intentional thinking along the way to take better care of myself and more clearly solve problems.

The rewards of everything I've shared with you in this book came from the confidence to:

- Embrace whatever might come my way;
- Look back and recognize my efforts as whole and good intentioned;
- Explore mistakes and let go of some obsessive obstacles that creep in.

Fire of Success Continues

Broken Bones and Beautiful New Beginnings

If my feet had eyes, they were blind to the four steps in front of them. I could have been cast as a ghost in a scary movie the way my arms flailed about in a footless flight down the stairs. Upon landing, a loud cracking sound echoed off the wall as my right foot smashed against ceramic tile. On second thought, I wasn't cut out to play a ghost. I hadn't had a drop to drink, so I couldn't even blame it on deadly last sip of wine.

The next day, Sean arrived with my first meal of the day. It was a Monday morning. Upon awakening, breakfast, lunch, and dinner had already been prepared for the day. With my foot propped up and an appropriate doze of medication, I was ready to feast on morning a homemade veggie burrito with hot sauce. This scene was the beginning of a beautiful relationship.

Upon first meeting with my daughters, it seemed history was repeating itself. Sean walked calmly over to my daughter to ask about a sewing project she was working on. I recalled my stepfather Bill so many years ago approaching me at around the same age to ask about a wolf spider report. Sean then asked my other daughter about the original story she was writing. Six years had passed since my divorce. A new meaningful chapter was unfolding.

More Broken Bones and Meaningful New Chapters

Once again, I must have been dreaming about landing a role as a clumsy ghost. Flailing my arms, I found myself flying down the stairs. This time, it was my left foot that cracked loudly against hard pavement. It was also the night before my wedding. Once again, I couldn't blame alcohol, as I hadn't had a drop to drink.

In my entire life, I had never broken a bone, unless you count the pinky toe I broke while doing a backflip in cheerleading. Now, I was affixing a faux diamond in an effort to 'bling' out a fitted boot. This boot would be sticking out of the bottom of a very lovely wedding gown. Although it was a bit disappointing, it was mostly confusing to the doctor and nurses that I was so calm and even cheerfully laughing alongside my soon-to-be husband.

This is one example of when I could have reacted negatively. Since I view these types of situations with more perspective, this unfortunate flight down the stairs led to a lot of laughs. Dancing on crutches while in a wedding gown is something we won't long forget!

A Peaceful Busy Schedule

While I'm busy with my speaking and coaching career, Sean is the CEO of a successful business. His biggest hobby is competing as a brown belt in international Brazilian Jiu Jitsu competitions. His commitment shows in the many gold medals he's earned over the years. He trains six nights a week after leaving his office from a full day of work. Why do I tell you all this? My husband is a high-performing example of living a peaceful, successful, and well-rounded life. People ask him, "How do you do it all?" My observation is that he has learned to ignite inner peace as a success calling. This is what you have been doing throughout this book.

Daily Peace and Harmony as Success

I was on the last sip of my first cup of hot coffee, fresh off the press. In everyday fashion, my cup was filled a second time by the hands of my husband, Sean. Although my foot was broken, my husband's behavior was not out of the ordinary. If I weren't practicing gratitude, I could have easily taken for granted the way that I was cared for and about.

What makes Sean uniquely special in my mind is his ability to approach his day calmly, with purpose, and without complaint. As a stepfather to my twin daughters, he is a perfectly suited complement to their dad. As role models, I believe both men offer extremely valuable lessons in perseverance.

Sean is the most genuinely humble person I know. Showing up in a humble way is a quality to which all of us should strive to arrive. He is a double Ivy League graduate, and he would be the last to tell you this. He speaks two languages outside of English and again wouldn't be the first to announce it. My citing his academic accomplishments has a point. The point is, although I admire his accomplishments, it is his day-to-day demonstration of peace and harmony that is most admirable. I strive to earn the degree of patience he practices.

You might think my husband's privileged, so no wonder he's successful. If this is on your mind, I would encourage you to exercise your beginner's mind about your definition of success. Your idea of others having it better could be holding you back. Remember, it is helpful to burn down judgements and conclusions you may have of others.

I am here to show you a different kind of success over education. It's everything we talk about in this book—the ability to be clear minded, ignite grace and gratitude, and reach levels of personal peace and harmony. To me, this is exactly how relationships thrive. Along with self-care, relationships should be nurtured and cared for consistently.

The following are my husband's daily actions in a formula that follows what we've been doing in this book. This is based on my personal observations and perception:

- **Focus** (morning gratitude practice): Decision to place focus and attention on what is most meaningful first (family, then work)

- **Flow** (clear-thinking/courage exercise): Acknowledge any fears and disappointments as they show up instead of dismissing or allowing them to ruin the day as a number-one rule of perseverance
- **Faith** (harmony, peace, and success): Choose to let go of what cannot be controlled and adopt a wholehearted belief that focus, and flow are the ongoing links to your success

A Peaceful, Balanced Life

After many years in the hectic corporate lifestyle, my husband Sean made the choice to face uncertainty in acquiring a company and taking on the role of CEO. As Chief Engineering Officer, his plate is never empty, of course.

In addition, he has a wife, two grown children, and two stepchildren with whom to spend quality time. Sean is responsible for his employees and must meet the demands of his daily duties. His active hobby is as a brown belt in Brazilian Jiu Jitsu. He competes yearly at the national and international level. Six nights a week, he trains after a full day of running a company.

How is this life any less hectic than the corporate style life? The answer, as I observe it, is his confidence in the ability to focus on the most meaningful things first. Sean succeeds in this every day, putting his self-care and biological and step family first, above all.

A Peaceful Busy Schedule

Preparing three meals a day for four people is my husband's daily habit prior to going to work. I promise you, I have little to do with the cooking in this house! He also does all the food shopping. The deal is that I do dishes and clean up. Even with all of these tasks, Sean still spends plenty of quality time with all of us. We never feel like he's working too much or playing too much.

I use my husband as an example of what's possible. I can imagine you are just as busy with many responsibilities. You most likely have a family or may be a caregiver to someone in your family. You might also be stressed and wondering if you'll ever catch a break. Remember this: it isn't about a break so much as focusing on the things that are most meaningful to you. If you're busy running around after kids, you can still create a life that doesn't have to be harried every day. As a mother of teenage twins, I can tell you this is possible.

Sean's choice to create a successful lifestyle as I've defined here includes the following five qualities:

- Daily Integrity
- Consistency
- Faithful/Action-Driven Mindset
- Focus
- Honorable Intent to Assist Others

Today, you can choose to piece together a better mindset. Today, anything is possible for you, including building in time for your family and being able to do your hobbies without the guilt. It can be done because I'm living it, and so are my friends. You can choose to live your life in survival-stressed mode or thriving-contributing mode. The choice really is yours. You don't have to prepare all your meals in the morning right out of the gate, or ever. The point is that you can create whatever lifestyle you want and get a whole hell of a lot done in the process.

ASK: In the area of daily integrity, what can I do to gain more trust from others?

In which areas do I practice the least consistency?

In the area of a faith and action-driven mindset, do I feel I could improve?

In the area of focus, what do I need to review?

In the area of honorable intent, is what I do each day for the purpose of helping others without asking anything in return?

In what areas do I feel I am my strongest self?

Daily Link to Success

When my daughters asked their stepfather if he was upset after losing a match during competition, he taught them what he learned from his coach: "There is no lose, only learn." This reminded me of Yoda's wisdom: "There is no try, only do."

Losses in your life can stop you from growing if you don't view them as learning opportunities. When we just go through life trying instead of doing, we have little chance of ever earning a gold medal in personal development. With permanent loss, we can still work to grieve properly so that we don't collapse in the face of any fallout major disappointments.

Ignite a New Beginning for Yourself

As we've gone through uncertainty, fear, doubt, and disappointment in this book, we arrive at your third level of peace, harmony, and success. At the end of our farewell to one another, you will view the fully built pyramid you worked to proactively develop habits of perseverance.

Today is your day to choose to ignite a new beginning for yourself outside of this book. I look forward to hearing about your progress.

Habit #4: Visual Trigger to Ignite Strong Habits

Light Up Yearly Success-Celebrate Your Progress

Adapted from Proactive Life Mastery Academy™ Online Training in Perseverance

Each year on your birthday, check back in with your progress over the year. Utilize the tools in this book to measure your progress over time. How did your strengths improve? How did your relationship with the Fiery Four change or improve? What will you do this year to set a new commitment to yourself?

Congratulations! You're onto your final habit to light up success! You've reached to the top of your pyramid of perseverance!

Pyramid of Perseverance:
AMC Proactive Levels to Success™

Adapted from Proactive Life Matters Academy™ Online Training in Perseverance
Personal Commitments Guide to Success Worksheet
Designed by, Amy McCann Coaching™

PART III SUMMARY

Congratulations! Drink in Your Progress! You've accomplished the following intelligent actions to ignite peace:

- ✓ Explored the Consequences of Stress
- ✓ Completed Inner Strengths Journey
- ✓ Completed Level-Two Perseverance: Intelligent Thinking, Planning, and Courage

- ✓ Participated in a Balanced Weekly Self-Care Exercise
- ✓ Committed to Weekly Courage Action Steps
- ✓ Gained Confidence and Awareness
- ✓ Completed Daily Mindset Shifts
- ✓ Learned About the Consequence of Worry
- ✓ Made a Commitment to Ongoing Success in Perseverance

YOU ARE A SUCCESS

Farewell (For Now)

As was said in my introduction, a fictional frog named Kermit once asked, "Who said that every wish would be heard and answered?" He often went back to his pond to reflect on life and contemplate the world around him. I'm glad you took this journey backward with me to the place from where I come. From my first decade of life to present, you stayed until the end. It is a show of open-minded curiosity to turn these pages. It is a confident measure of personal success that you invested time to look within yourself to build strength through uncertainty.

As you move forward through uncertainty, take a moment to reflect upon these ideas:

> A clear-thinking vision through uncertainty is rarely sparked or realized until you've built a foundation and purpose to live in grace.
>
> Daily grace is achieved when you work to ignite gratitude.
>
> Strength and courage begin by igniting a commitment to self-care.
>
> Curiosity, imagination, and a beginner's mind are three persevering tools that can be easily practiced igniting inner peace, and harmony.

When you become more aware, mindful, and connected to yourself and others, life naturally becomes less stressful, more joyful, and ultimately, more successful. When you can succeed in daily life, you will meet any big disaster head on with greater confidence and humor. You will also have a clear mind to create new vision for yourself and realize your dreams.

As I feel my level of gratitude rise, the time has come to lower the heat on my keyboard and say farewell for now. Before we part, I have one more gift for you. In return for engaging with my first published book, I invite you to sign up for two complimentary tickets to my next LIVE speaking event. Please email my team at the link below.

Let's now officially part as more grateful, courageous, and masterful peace workers who made it through uncertainty. It has been fiery journey getting through the burns and scars that uncertainty, doubt, fear, and disappointment can bring. Together, we stuck it out. Through it all, you persevered. From the beginning, and in the end, you are a success.

~Persevere to Succeed~
Amy McCann

amy@3DStressSolutionsCoach.com

ACKNOWLEDGEMENTS

I wish to thank those who brought forth my voice these past four years as well as those who helped bring this book to life and into the light.

To Sharon Livingston, my mentor, and friend. You are one of those rare people who has a gift of helping others polish the best parts of themselves to help them become who they are meant to be. Thank you for being my mentor and noticing the shiny parts of me. We met when I was going through a difficult time and you handled me gently, helping me build upon my strengths. Everyone needs someone through tough times, and you helped me find my voice again. It is because of you I was able to repurpose what is inside of me, to help others as a professional coach. You helped me access the gifts inside of me and now I've put them together in this very first book. I am truly grateful for you.

To Rodney Long, my fellow coach, and friend. A few years ago, while sitting in a training, you handed me a note. I have kept that note and have it memorized. I refer to your words on those days I have trouble bringing forth my voice. Your note reads: Always allow your unique you to shine. Never hold back your unique message. You are here for a purpose. Don't let the child stand in the way of the purpose. Thank you so much, my friend, for knowing exactly what to say and why it needed to be said at the time. Your message will forever live with me.

To Laurie-Ann Murabito, my speaking coach, friend, and fellow author. You are the person responsible for encouraging me to light a fire under my own butt to get this book written! Just a year ago, you mingled with me casually at a networking event and then found a way to get me to say I would have a book written and published by the Fall of 2018. It has been my honor to have you as my hired coach these past months and for seeing me through to completion of this book. I can't wait to share the stage with you as a speaker. Thank you for all of your support and help in building my momentum and progress.

To Susan Wall, my best friend in the world. You can now call me a fellow author! Of course, I wrote about you in this book, but I wanted to acknowledge all you've done to make this book come to life. From designing the cover to offering to do the digital and print versions of this book. You saved me a huge headache, and I can't thank you enough.

To my inner book circle of readers, thank you for investing even a minute to read all of the terrible first drafts. This final version may not be perfect, but it's about a process, isn't it? I am so grateful you all signed up to show me support. Thank you for the honest feedback which is greatly appreciated.

Finally, I wish to acknowledge and thank PavEDITa https://www.pavedita.com/services for last minute edits and support.

Last but not least, I wish to thank my ex-husband Kevin, who gave me the two greatest gifts in the world, our twin daughters, Emma and Annalise. Thank you for being a great father to them, and for helping me help others through all you've taught me about perseverance.

ABOUT THE AUTHOR

At eight years old, uncertainty struck following a devastating house fire that left Amy's brother badly burned. In her early twenties, uncertainty struck again after her fiancé suffered a permanent spinal cord injury. Two decades of battling stress as a full-time caregiver taught her there is a better way to persevere through major life changes.

Today, Amy is a professional speaker and Certified High Performance Coach. She is a graduate of the American Academy of Dramatic Arts and also holds a Bachelor of Science in psychology, specializing in stress associated with major life transition. Amy helps others step onto a new state of courage and confidence in the face of overwhelming uncertainty. Amy believes a successful life begins with a commitment to self-care and mastery in the art of perseverance.

www.ingramcontent.com/pod-product-compliance
Lightning Source LLC
LaVergne TN
LVHW051229080426
835513LV00016B/1489

* 9 7 8 1 9 4 1 8 5 2 2 1 7 *